Understanding Character Education

Understanding Character Education

Approaches, Applications, and Issues

Paul Watts, Michael Fullard, and Andrew Peterson

Open University Press

Open University Press
McGraw Hill
8th Floor, 338 Euston Road
London
England
NW1 3BH

email: enquiries@openup.co.uk
world wide web: www.openup.co.uk

First edition published 2021

A catalogue record of this book is available from the British Library

ISBN-13: 9780335250516
ISBN-10: 0335250513
eISBN: 9780335250523

Library of Congress Cataloging-in-Publication Data
CIP data applied for

Typeset by Transforma Pvt. Ltd., Chennai, India

At a time when Character Education has become one of the most popular frameworks to understand the moral development of children and young people in schools, this book offers an extensive introduction to Character Education that will be of great use to students, teacher educators and practitioners. The authors, experts and key advocates of Character Education succeed in providing a theoretical text underpinned with a range of reflective and case study activities that clearly connect with up-to-date policy and practice in schools in England.

Edda Sant, Senior Lecturer, Manchester Metropolitan University, UK

Wherever you, your school or organisation is at in terms of understanding what Character Education is and how to effectively implement it, this book is essential. It provides extensive practical guidance on how to deliver transformative character education, while being grounded in pedagogical research and theory. The outstanding practice seen in schools and organisations of character is all reflected in this accessible and truly engaging book. Highly recommended for all leaders and practitioners dedicated to enabling children and young people to flourish through the development of good character.

Tom Haigh, CEO, Association for Character Education

Understanding Character Education manages to bridge that difficult gap between research and practical application in such a wonderful way. The seven chapters take distinct elements of applying theory to practice, a mix in interesting case studies and thoughtful self-reflection stimuli to provide something of a how-to guide for educators implementing Character Education in schools. It is sufficiently accessible to be useful to those new to education but contains sufficient depth to challenge those further down the Character Education development journey. I wish Chapter 2: The Character of the Teacher was made a compulsory read for every person working in a UK school; that would be transformational.

Nat Parnell, Regional Director, United Learning

Built around a neo-Aristotelian approach to Character Education, this principled and finely argued book offers a compelling approach to practice. At the heart of the book is a belief that human flourishing and the development of the virtues can and should be embedded deeply into schools; chapter-by-chapter the authors make the case for a language of character and virtues, offer new insight into teacher professionality and show how a richly infused learning environment can be created. The authors offer a reconceptualization of behaviour for learning and

for Character Education across and beyond the curriculum. With argu-
ments grounded in theory, this invaluable book offers a contextually
layered means by which practice can be developed with integrity.

Professor Hazel Bryan, Dean of the School of Education and Professional
Development, University of Huddersfield, UK

We often think that schools have a responsibility to get their pupils
college-ready or career-ready. The signal achievement of Understanding Character Education *is the authors' clarion call that schools also*
have a responsibility to graduate students who are character and citi-
zen-ready. I can't wait to introduce new teachers to the beautifully
written case studies and reflective activities.

Arthur Schwartz, President, Character.org

The personal and social development of pupils has never been more
important; yet finding 'space' in amongst the other pressures and
expectations put upon teachers for such focus is challenging. Teachers
wish to spend more time focusing on developing the whole child but
cannot seem to find this time. Understanding Character Education
invites you to think about the importance of personal and social devel-
opment through the concept of character education; offering tools and
approaches that will enable you to create the space to develop pupils'
virtues within and across the curriculum, as well as beyond the school
gates. Understanding Character Education *reminds us that a core part*
of our role is to enable pupils to function and flourish as people, as
friends and as members of their communities. Punctuated with reflec-
tion activities and case studies, Understanding Character Education
provides opportunities for critical reflective thinking whilst providing
real life contexts that underpin the theory and research presented. A
must read for all trainee teachers of any phase.

Catherine Carden, Director of Learning and Teaching, Faculty of Arts
Humanities & Education, Canterbury Christ Church University, UK

Understanding Character Education *is a tour de force of the theory,*
practice and application of character education. Comprehensive,
thoughtful and eminently practical, this book is a must read for any-
one who takes education and schooling seriously. Watts, Fullard and
Peterson provide a nuanced account of the conceptual frameworks
animating authentic character education, and their case studies of
practitioners from around the world provide a wonderful window into
what effective character education looks like. A refreshing and hopeful
guide to revitalizing school leadership and culture.

Dr. Karen Bohlin, Senior Scholar, Boston University Center
for Character & Social Responsibility

Contents

Figures, tables, boxes, and case studies

Acknowledgements

As with any book project, the production of the physical product is the outcome of a long process. We have a number of colleagues and friends to thank for their support and without whom the process would not have reached fruition. Our colleagues at Open University Press – Eleanor Christie, Beth Summers, and Zoe Osman – have been a joy to work with. Their confidence in the book and ongoing advice (and patience!) at every stage has been very much appreciated. We also owe a big debt of gratitude to the authors of the case studies that appear throughout the book. Quite literally, the book would not be what it is without their input. Their work on character education has inspired us and, we know, will continue to inspire us over the coming years.

We thank all of our colleagues at the Jubilee Centre for Character and Virtues for their ongoing academic friendship. While any errors in content and judgement are clearly our own, we also owe our gratitude to those who were kind enough to offer comments and advice on parts of – or on the whole of – the manuscript: James Arthur, Kristján Kristjánsson, Tom Harrison, Peter Oldham, and Julie Taylor. Finally, we would like to thank our families for their patience and care as we researched, drafted, and finalised the manuscript.

Introduction

As all teachers and other staff who work in schools know, supporting pupils'[1] personal and social development lies at the heart of education. Though other aims of education and schooling are also evident, no school or teacher can avoid their role in enabling pupils to function and flourish as people, as friends, and as members of various communities. At times, this work becomes constrained as other pressures and needs redirect schools' work or take priority. A leading and often-cited example of such pressures is the 'measurement' of academic learning and progression through tests and examinations. Many will be well aware of the impact that tests and examinations, particularly those regarded as 'high-stakes', exert. Over recent years, many school leaders, teachers, and others interested in education have suggested that certain tests can take away from or neglect the true academic and personal worth of pupils. In one such letter that made headline news – sent by a headteacher in England to primary school pupils before their Standard Assessment Tests (SATs) – it was made clear to the pupils that the tests could not reflect everything that makes each one of them 'special and unique'. Among a range of qualities cited as not being covered by the SATs were, 'they do not know that your friends can count on you to be there for them,' and 'that you are kind, trustworthy and thoughtful and that every day you try to be the very best person that you can be'. The letter ended by saying, 'Remember "Educating the mind without educating the heart is no education at all" as Aristotle said'.[2]

As this letter highlights, education is about much more than a life of academic learning, tests, and examinations – though these are, of course, important. Education is fundamentally about helping pupils to develop in a holistic sense – academically, personally, and socially. Yet, precisely what it means to develop personally and socially can be interpreted in a number of ways and can include a number of different elements. Consider the following questions: What does 'personal and social development' mean? How does 'personal development' relate to 'social development'? What is the extent of a school's legitimate role in pupils' personal and social development? Should schools work with families and communities in shaping pupils' personal and social development, or should they also seek to challenge and critique other socialising factors? Should personal and social development be limited to cognition, emotions, and/or attitudes? How do schools support pupils' personal and social development without indoctrinating or being overly paternalistic? How can schools teach pupils to be critical and reflective about their personal and social development while also encouraging them to share core values or virtues? How does the role and focus of schools change so far as pupils' personal and social development is concerned, as pupils move through the age ranges?

These questions are not easy to answer, but your initial responses will say something important about the sort of approach to pupils' personal and social development you would advocate. In this book, you will be introduced to character education as an approach to pupils' personal and social development. As will become clear through the words, activities, and case studies you read throughout, we believe that centring on character provides schools and teachers – and the pupils, families, and communities they serve – with the basis for an intentional, explicit, and cohesive approach. It should be noted from the outset, too, that there are different approaches that can give meaning and intention to pupils' personal and social development, including positive education, social and emotional learning, human rights education, and education for citizenship. In some schools these other approaches to personal and social development work alongside character education, while in others they provide a distinct alternative.

We define character and character education, and say more about some of these other approaches, in more detail in Chapter 1, but from the outset it is important to realise that character education is one form of what, historically and broadly, has been termed *moral* or *values education*. There has been something of a revival of interest in character education in a number of countries, including in the United States since the 1990s and, more recently, in the United Kingdom (particularly, though not exclusively, in England). Character education is, however, not new and should be understood instead as a 'perennial aim of education' (Arthur, 2020: 1; see also Howard et al., 2004). Indeed, Arthur (2020: 8) argues that 'the formation of character could be said to be the aim that all general education has set out to achieve'. Think here, for example, about your own goals and expectations as a teacher. It is likely that these connect in some way to a desire to help children to develop and express core aspects of their character – to be kind, to be curious, and so on. However, as Arthur – and other writers on character education that we introduce in this book – suggest, the formation of character as an aim of education has at times remained implicit rather than explicit. In addition, character education has also been the subject of criticism and dispute concerning the form and focus it should take in schools – especially those forms of character education that take a remedial rather than aspirational approach (Kristjánsson, 2013; Jubilee Centre, 2017). As the pages of this book will attest, we believe that where schools take a positive, intentional, and explicit approach, character education can transform educational contexts and relationships, affirming the difference that education can and does make to pupils, schools, and communities.

About this book

The aim of this book is for you to explore and engage critically with the key ideas, methods, and practices involved in character education. Effective character education requires the synthesis of various aspects of education, teaching, and learning. Recognising the importance of this synthesis, the book is structured around the following seven chapters:

In addition to the main text, each chapter includes a variety of features to help you navigate your way through the ideas, themes, and practices examined. These include:

- **chapter objectives** to help you understand the core focus and intentions of each chapter
- **reflective activities** to help you to pause, to think more deeply about particular ideas and issues, and to consider how the practices described are, or could be, applied in your own contexts
- **case studies** to help you to understand how character education is approached and implemented by educators in and beyond schools
- **annotated further readings** to help you take a closer and more detailed look at the methods, applications, and issues covered in the chapters.

As you work through the book we ask that you bear three, related, considerations in mind. First, in most educational contexts, pupils' personal and social development more generally, and character education more specifically, can represent:

1 a general aim of education and schooling
2 a statutory subject within the formal curriculum
3 a subject within the curriculum implemented within individual schools
4 a goal or theme that sits across the curriculum
5 an outcome of extra-curricular activities.

Indeed, in all contexts pupils' personal and social development and character education involve a mixture of these processes. Throughout the book we make use of the distinction drawn in the Jubilee Centre for Character and Virtues' *A Framework for Character Education in Schools* (2017: 9) between character caught, taught, and sought:

- **Caught:** the school community of both staff and students provide the example, culture, and inspirational influence in a positive ethos that motivates and promotes character development.

- **Taught:** the school provides educational experiences in and out of the classroom that equip students with the language, knowledge, understanding, skills, and attributes that enable character development.
- **Sought:** the school provides varied opportunities that generate the formation of personal habits and character commitments. These help students over time to seek, desire, and freely pursue their character development.

Second, and linked to the first consideration, while some educational contexts have a formal set of standards for character education – here Singapore provides a good example – in many contexts schools and teachers work with non-binding standards and frameworks (see, for example, the *Character & Social-Emotional Development Model Standards*[3] produced by Character.org, or the 2019 *Character Education Framework Guidance* produced by the Department for Education in England), including those they develop themselves.

Third, because of its very nature, character education must be guided by the context in which it occurs, shaped that is by the nature and needs of the schools, pupils, and communities involved. We return to this point at various times throughout the book, arguing that while there are some core ideas and practices that underpin all effective character education, there is not a 'one-size-fits-all' version that will work for every context, in every school and – importantly – for all pupils. Instead, schools and teachers who take a character-based approach to pupils' personal and social development will need to take the general principles, ideas, and vocabulary and make these work for their contexts, for their schools, and for their pupils.

While we examine a range of ideas, issues, and processes involved in adopting a character-based approach to pupils' personal and social development, we are aware that no book can be truly exhaustive in its coverage. This is an introductory book in which we aim to introduce you to character education and the impact a character-based approach can have in schools. In the final chapter, we point you in the direction of further ideas and resources that can help you to develop your understanding and own practice further. In the meantime, we hope that you enjoy your engagement with the contents of this book – and that it stimulates both your thinking about and your practice in taking a character-based approach to pupils' personal and social development.

Notes

1 Readers should note that we use the term 'pupils' in preference to 'students' throughout the book.
2 https://www.theguardian.com/education/2018/may/15/these-tests-only-measure-a-little-bit-of-you-the-teachers-letters-that-go-viral
3 https://www.character.org/model-standards

1 Character and character education

Introduction

This book adopts a character-based approach to pupils' personal and social development, examining and setting out key ideas about, and methods for, cultivating character. Ideas of character and character education are ancient in origin, but have found a renewed commitment within and across a range of contexts over the last two decades. Over this period, various governments, educational institutions, education organisations, and academics from a range of disciplines (including philosophy, psychology, sociology, and education) have developed a real interest in, and commitment to, character education. This interest in character education has taken different forms, with advocates of similar but not identical approaches seeking to contribute to educational thinking and practice in the area.

In this chapter, you will be introduced to key definitions of character and character education as well as to related concepts and approaches (positive education, social and emotional learning). In addition, the chapter gives an overview of key elements of character education, and starts to familiarise you with some of the key principles of effective practice in the field.

Chapter Objectives

By the end of this chapter, you should have:

- Considered the meaning of character and character education
- Examined briefly positive education and social and emotional learning as similar, though not identical, approaches to character education
- Started to develop your understanding of the main elements of character education, including key principles.

Defining character and character education

The term 'character' derives from the ancient Greek word *kharaktḗr*, meaning to engrave or make a mark. Over time, the meaning of the concept 'character' developed to refer to the 'mark' or 'qualities' of a person, and today character can be generally understood to refer to 'a set of personal traits or dispositions that produce specific moral emotions, inform motivation and guide conduct' (Jubilee Centre, 2017: 2). This definition highlights that our character is part of (though not necessarily all of) who we are as a human being. Our character is often understood and appraised – by ourselves and by others – through the actions we take and the qualities we exhibit. We can see this through the everyday, commonplace vocabulary of character. When we talk about family, friends, colleagues, public figures, and others, we often define them through their qualities – whether they are kind, honest, trustworthy, for example. Equally, when someone makes a mistake, we might say that the person's conduct was 'out of character'. In addition, there are some qualities that we may view as being particularly important for given roles (being a kind friend, being a patient teacher, being a compassionate nurse, being an honest lawyer, being a brave soldier, and so on).

Some qualities – those that are truly ingrained in our character – will be deeper and more central to 'who we are' than other qualities that we hold less deeply or dearly. In his book *The Road to Character* (2016), David Brooks distinguishes between 'résumé' and 'eulogy' virtues, and it is worth considering how Brooks casts these two types and the condition of contemporary society. Brooks defines résumé virtues as 'the skills that you bring to the job market' that 'contribute to external success'. In contrast, the eulogy virtues are more deeply rooted in our character. These are the virtues that 'get talked about at your funeral ... whether you are kind, brave, honest or faithful; what kind of relationships you have formed' (2016: i). Brooks reflects that while most would agree that it is the eulogy virtues that are more important, our current lives, and crucially our education systems, tend to focus much more on résumé virtues. For Brooks this means that most people have 'clearer strategies' for being successful in their careers than for developing 'a profound character'.

Consider your own experience in schools. Was more emphasis placed on the résumé virtues or on the eulogy virtues? Which of the two was emphasised more explicitly? Now consider what you would deem most important for your own child or for children more generally – résumé virtues or eulogy virtues? For a final reflection on this point, consider the role of teachers – should they be more concerned with developing résumé or eulogy virtues? These are not easy questions to answer, and of course education is not a concrete choice *between* résumé and eulogy. A good, well-rounded education will help pupils to develop *both* résumé and eulogy virtues. Brooks' point, however, is that education systems today focus on the former much more than the latter and that this, somewhat paradoxically, is contrary to what, deep down, most of us believe to be the more important virtues.

All schools and educational settings, whether consciously or unconsciously, impact on the qualities and dispositions of children and young people – that is, the sorts of people they are. In rather general terms, *character education* is the conscious process of cultivating worthwhile and positive dispositions – these positive dispositions are referred to throughout this book as *character virtues* or *character strengths*. Some important definitions of character education include the following:

[Character education is] the deliberate effort by schools, families and communities to help young people understand, care about, and act upon core ethical values. (Character Education Partnership, cited in Lickona, 1996: 93)

Character education includes all explicit and implicit educational activities that help young people develop positive personal strengths called virtues. (Jubilee Centre, 2017: 2)

Character education holds out the hope of what a person can be as opposed to what they are. Character education is not the same as behaviour control, discipline, training, or indoctrination, it is much broader and has more ambitious goals ... Character is an inclusive term for the individual as a whole. (Arthur, 2014: 53)

[Character education is] the intentional attempt in schools to foster the development of students' psychological characteristics that motivate and enable them to act in ethical, democratic, and socially effective and productive ways. (Berkowitz et al., 2012: 72)

The expanded definition of character education offered by the Jubilee Centre for Character and Virtues (2017: 2) includes the suggestion that:

character education is more than just a subject. It has a place in the culture and functions of families, classrooms, schools and other institutions. Character education is about helping students grasp what is ethically important in situations and how they act for the right reasons, such that they become more autonomous and reflective in the practice of virtue.

As these definitions attest, character education as a concept is a deliberate and intentional educational effort. Yet, and at the same time, it is important to remember that all educators have an impact on the character of the children and young people with whom they work – whether consciously or unconsciously, positively or negatively. In other words, character education is not optional! As we will consistently suggest throughout this book, meaningful and effective character education is intentional, clearly focused, and concentrates on morally and socially worthwhile qualities. Alongside other aspects of teaching – such as supporting pupils' academic development and preparing pupils for employability – the development of active, informed, and engaged citizens who form positive relationships with others sits as a core aim of most education and schooling systems.

The formation of children and young people who are kind, honest, curious, and determined is not only central to what it means to be a 'good' teacher, but is often what motivates teachers to enter their profession in the first place. This said, the role schools and teachers have in pupils' personal and social development is not one that they hold alone. The personal and indeed social development of young people is an endeavour shared by schools with families, friends, peers, neighbourhoods, communities, and various media. An important and ongoing task, therefore, is to be constantly mindful about how these various 'partners' in personal and social development support and/or constrain the work of schools and teachers in this regard. Once we accept that schools and teachers are inherently involved in shaping the character of their pupils, the emphasis changes from whether this happens to how and why it happens. This shift is one from an unintentional, unplanned, and unsystematic approach to an approach that is intentional, planned, and systematic. In the rest of this chapter, we introduce you to various foundational aspects of character education. These aspects underpin and shape the exploration of the 'how' and 'why' of a character-based approach to pupils' personal and social development in the following chapters.

Different, but related, approaches to personal and social development

Marvin Berkowitz (2016) has referred to the field of moral education as a 'semantic minefield'. Part of the reason for this minefield is that key terms and concepts are often understood and used in different ways. In addition, a variety of terms and concepts are used for what – if not necessarily identical – are similar approaches. In visualising the state of the field, Berkowitz (2016) highlights that 'the terminology varies geographically and historically. And there are many overlapping terms used: moral education, values education, character education, civic education, citizenship education, democratic education, moralogy, social-emotional learning, positive psychology, etc.'. Also, reflecting on the field of research on moral education, Kristján Kristjánsson (2017: 342) has pondered whether we are best viewing these different terms and approaches as a 'hopeless hotchpotch' or a 'healthy melting pot'. In the reality of everyday schools, teachers and other educators are more likely to be working with and across a range of these approaches.

In this book, we present a broadly neo-Aristotelian approach to character education. This approach is one which draws on key ideas from Aristotle – the importance of character and developing virtues, for example – but which seeks to update Aristotle's thought in light of contemporary ideas and evidence (for a detailed overview of 'Aristotelian character education', see Kristjánsson, 2015). From a neo-Aristotelian perspective, character education is concerned with the education and development of *virtues*. Virtues are stable, positive traits of character that are morally worthwhile, educable, and help us to live a good life. Virtues are also identity-conferring, in the sense that they define the person who possesses them (they are honest, they are kind, and so on). We commend those traits when we see them in others – praising them for being just, kind, honest, brave, humble, and so on. The focus on character and virtues within character education draws on the wider tradition in moral philosophy of *virtue ethics*. Virtue ethics itself is ancient in origin but witnessed a revival in the latter half of the twentieth century as a response to two dominant moral theories which broadly understood the rightness and wrongness of actions in terms of their consequences (consequentialism) or the following of given rules (deontology). While it appears a peculiar direction for modern moral philosophy to take in returning to ancient thinkers, modern virtue ethicists take a neo-Aristotelian approach which is regarded as applicable within, and reflective of, modern society (Hursthouse, 1999). Rather than being concerned primarily with consequences or rules, virtue ethicists are interested in the moral character of the agent (or person) and what it means to be good (virtuous). In his writings, Aristotle emphasised a small set of virtues that characterised a good person, but more commonly a larger, and more contemporary, range of virtues is used to help us understand what it means to be good and to live a good life. This larger range of virtues can also be found in how schools frame their implementation of character education. Later on in this chapter we say more about these virtues (see Table 1.2).

Two other ideas that we return to at various parts of this book form a core part of an Aristotelian approach to character education:

1 *Phronesis* – which translates to 'good sense' or 'practical wisdom'. Practical wisdom is the overarching virtue that is 'developed through experience and critical reflection, which enables us to perceive, know, desire, and act with good sense. This includes discerning deliberative action in situations where virtues collide' (Jubilee Centre, 2017: 5). Though more research is needed regarding how practical wisdom is educated, it is generally thought that practical wisdom develops through habituation, experience, and critical intra- and inter-personal reflection (see Chapter 7).
2 *Eudaimonia* – which translates to 'happiness' or 'human flourishing'. According to Aristotle, virtues are necessary not only for flourishing but also constitute human flourishing. In other words, humans flourish when they possess and enact moral and intellectual virtue(s). Indeed, for Aristotle possession of a virtue *entails* enactment. When humans possess the virtues fully they realise their full potential (Kristjánsson, 2020).

It is interesting to note that the concepts of practical wisdom and human flourishing were, until fairly recently, generally only discussed in philosophical circles. In recent years, these terms have not only entered the conceptual vocabulary of psychologists but, and more importantly for this book, they are increasingly used to frame and guide research and practice conducted within schools.

While some approaches to pupils' personal and moral development focus on specific capacities, such as how well a child can reason or their emotional states, character education understands virtues as comprised of a number of components. The Jubilee Centre for Character and Virtues' (2017: 8) framework presents these components as:

- Virtue Perception: Noticing situations involving or standing in need of the virtues
- Virtue Knowledge and Understanding: Understanding the meaning of the virtue term and why the virtue is important

- Virtue Emotion: Feeling the right virtue-relevant emotion in the right situation in the right way
- Virtue Identity: Understanding oneself as strongly committed to the virtues
- Virtue Motivation: Having a strong desire to act on the virtues
- Virtue Reasoning: Discernment and deliberative action about virtues, including in situations where virtues conflict or collide
- Virtue Action and Practice: Doing the right thing in the right way

Effective character education needs to attend to the development of each of these components. You might immediately recognise that, particularly for young children, bringing together and balancing these various components – and indeed deciding the order in which to teach them – is not an easy educational task! We say much more about character education in the remaining sections of this chapter. Next, we introduce you to two similar, though not identical, approaches to pupils' personal and social development.

Positive education

Positive education refers to educational approaches that translate key principles of *positive psychology* within education and teaching. Much like the field of character education, positive education is a broad discipline with various and varied approaches and emphases. Two of the founders of positive psychology, Martin Seligman and Mihaly Csikszentmihalyi, define positive psychology as 'the scientific study of positive human functioning and flourishing on multiple levels that include the biological, personal, relational, institutional, cultural, and global dimensions of life' (2000: 5). A core basic principle of positive psychology is the importance of developing a positive mindset and sense of self-efficacy – and these lie at the heart of positive education. This simple definition noted, two main schools of thought exist within positive psychology/positive education (though we treat these two schools here as indicative and recognise that there are overlaps between them). One broad school of positive psychology/positive education – symbolised by Peterson and Seligman's *Character Strengths and Virtues* (2004) – recognises the intrinsic worth of certain characteristics, notably virtues. While it is not identical to (neo)Aristotelian character education (it does not, for example, emphasise practical wisdom to the same extent) there are clear overlaps. The other school of thought is more narrow, focusing almost entirely on instrumentally valuable performance 'skills'. Through books such as Angela Duckworth's *Grit: The Power of Passion and Perseverance* (2016) and Paul Tough's *How Children Succeed: Confidence, Curiosity and the Hidden Power of Character* (2012), this more narrow branch within positive psychology has attracted a lot of interest in education, with terms such as wellbeing, resilience, and determination now part of the common lexicon of schools.[1] We might say that this narrower school within positive education is more interested in the 'résumé' virtues.

Widening out once more, the vision of the International Positive Education Network (IPEN) reads, 'we believe in a world where wellbeing, character and resilience education are core elements of the global ecosystem'.[2] In this vision we can see the commitment to two terms more commonly associated with positive education than character education – wellbeing and resilience – alongside the term character. IPEN's definition of positive education reads: 'Positive Education is the application of the science of Positive Psychology and related fields within an educational setting to encourage students, faculty, schools, universities and communities to flourish'. Part of the difficulty in drawing clear and fixed lines between these two schools of thought, and indeed between positive education and character education, is that at times they use similar terms – we are back to the 'semantic minefield' again!

One of the core models of positive education that has been used as a basis for education practice is Seligman's (2011; see also Norrish, 2015) PERMA(H)[3] model of happiness.

P – **Positive emotion:** building positive emotional responses
E – **Engagement:** engaging fully in testing tasks
R – **Relationships:** positive connections to and with others that give life meaning
M – **Meaning:** a sense of something larger than one's self
A – **Accomplishments:** pursuing achievement and success for its own sake
(H) – **Health:** positive physical activity, diet, and rest

Reflective Activity 1.1: Schools as supportive and/or restrictive environments

Think about a school you have a good level of knowledge about. This might be a school you work at, have spent time at, or could even be a school you attended. Using the PERMA(H) model as a basis, consider how the school as a whole – its culture and ethos, its curriculum, its teaching, the relationships between teachers and pupils, the relationships between pupils, and so on – supported and/or restricted each element. Like any organisation, schools are complex and it is likely that some aspects of a school's work will be supportive and other aspects will be restrictive.

Similarly influential, particularly in the measurement of virtues, is the VIA Inventory of Strengths (Peterson and Seligman, 2004). The VIA-IS consists of 24 character strengths, sub-divided as followed into six categories of virtue:

1 Wisdom and knowledge (creativity, curiosity, judgement, love of learning, perspective)
2 Courage (bravery, honesty, perseverance, zest)
3 Humanity (kindness, love, social intelligence)
4 Justice (fairness, leadership, teamwork)

5 Temperance (forgiveness, humility, prudence, self-regulation)
6 Transcendence (appreciation of beauty and excellence, gratitude, hope, humour, spirituality).

The VIA-IS provides a way to measure the self-perceived character strengths of individuals, who complete an online measure and can receive a report on their 'signature strengths'. One way that schools and other educational settings have adopted the VIA-IS is to use it as a basis for identifying the character strengths of pupils and to plan and assess educational interventions on this basis.

Reflective Activity 1.2: What are your character strengths? Take the test!

A free version of the VIA-IS can be taken at https://www.viacharacter.org/survey/account/register. Take the test and discover what it suggests about your character strengths. Are the strengths ones that you recognise in yourself? Are they strengths your family and friends would recognise in you?

Social and emotional learning

There are also some similarities and overlaps between character education and social and emotional learning. Originally based on the psychological theory of emotional intelligence (see, for example, Goleman, 1995), social and emotional learning is now a relatively common feature of education and schooling, although once again differences exist in both theoretical and practical approaches – for example, in how the amoral concept of emotional intelligence connects to moral dispositions and virtues (Kristjánsson, 2006a). The US-based Collaborative for Academic, Social, and Emotional Learning (CASEL) define social and emotional learning (SEL) as:

> the process through which all young people and adults acquire and apply the knowledge, skills, and attitudes to develop healthy identities, manage emotions and achieve personal and collective goals, feel and show empathy for others, establish and maintain supportive relationships, and make responsible and caring decisions.[4]

CASEL's (2020) framework highlights five competencies of SEL: self-awareness, self-management, social awareness, relationship skills, and responsible decision-making.

Schools focus on SEL in a variety of ways. In the same vein as research on character education and positive education, research and supportive literature on SEL emphasises the importance of approaches that are 'planned, systematic, monitored, improved, and refined over time' (Weissberg and O'Brien, 2004: 94; see also Snyder, 2014). A Guidance Report produced for primary schools by the Education Endowment Foundation (2019: 5) in England underlines a number of positive impacts research suggests SEL can have:

- improved social and emotional skills;
- improved academic performance;
- improved attitudes, behaviour and relationships with peers;
- reduced emotional distress (student depression, anxiety, stress and social withdrawal);
- reduced levels of bullying;
- reduced conduct problems; and
- improved school connection.

The Guidance Report also makes clear that, within schools, SEL can be implemented at the level of the whole school, the level of a whole class, and/or at a more targeted level of individual pupils or groups of pupils. To guide and support this work, six key recommendations, based on the evidence available, are given: that SEL skills are taught explicitly; that SEL skills are integrated and modelled through teaching; that SEL programmes are carefully planned; that curriculum approaches to SEL are Sequential, Active, Focused, and Explicit; that SEL is reinforced through a whole-school ethos; and, that the implementation of SEL is planned, supported, and monitored (2019: 8–9).

As will become clear as you make your way through the pages of this book, these six recommendations are not at all dissimilar from the cornerstones of effective practice in character education, or indeed of positive education. All three place an emphasis on: the holistic development of children; the importance of a committed leadership; the need for an intentional and planned approach; the value of a supportive culture and ethos; a combination of direct teaching and wider enrichment activities; and the development of intrapersonal and interpersonal qualities. In addition, and as we have mentioned previously, there is some common (if not always shared) language – flourishing, emotional learning, decision-making, and wellbeing. In practice, schools may well incorporate aspects of all three, whether consciously or not, and your own work is likely to be shaped by the decisions of the educational setting in which you work.

This said, and recognising that the 'semantic minefield' and overlapping ground make the territory of clear and fixed distinctions somewhat precarious, there are some important differences in emphasis that should be highlighted. We detail some of these differences in Table 1.1.

The fundamentals of character education

Throughout this book, you will be introduced to a range of theoretical ideas, empirical research, and professional practice that examine and demonstrate approaches to character education. In this section, we outline some of the 'fundamentals' of character education that we will return to at various stages.

Table 1.1 Key differences between positive education, social and emotional learning, and character education

	Positive education tends towards	Social and emotional learning tends towards	Character education tends towards
Theoretical underpinnings	Informed by positive psychology	Informed by various theories of emotional development	Informed by Aristotelian theory
Qualities emphasised/ terminology used	Strengths/positive experiences/virtues depending on intrinsic or instrumental emphasis	Skills	Virtues
Main emphasis is on	The development of a range of character strengths/positive experiences, or the development of performance virtues, such as grit, resilience, and optimism	Emotional development, including understanding emotions, self-efficacy, and self-awareness	Moral and intellectual virtues, such as honesty, compassion, curiosity, and open-mindedness
Guiding quality/ virtue	No guiding quality, with wisdom and knowledge as one of six categories of virtue	No guiding quality, with responsible decision-making as one of five competencies	Practical wisdom as a guiding meta-virtue
Interest in wider social structures and processes	Emphasises individual emotions, resilience, and wellbeing	Emphasises social awareness based on emotional relationships with others	Emphasises that virtues are individually adjusted and social in nature
Ultimate goal	Subjective wellbeing/flourishing	Improved social and emotional skills/emotional intelligence	Human flourishing that is both subjectively guided but objectively worthwhile

These are core principles and ideas that, in addition to those that you have already been introduced to, underpin effective character education: the building blocks of character; the language of character; and key principles of effective practice in character education.

The building blocks of character

As you work further through this book, it will become more and more clear that character education can be approached in many different ways, and comprises many different elements. It is often the case that certain schools place rather more emphasis on some of these elements than others, whether through a deliberate choice (to reflect the age of the pupils; the expertise of staff; the needs of the community) or not. Figure 1.1 presents the 'building blocks of character' (Jubilee Centre, 2017: 5). Within this, four 'types' of virtues are set out: intellectual virtues, moral virtues, civic virtues, and performance virtues (see also Baehr, 2017; Shields, 2011). You will also see that each of these types of virtue feeds into practical wisdom – the meta-virtue we introduced in the first section of this chapter – and that, in turn, these all aim at individual and societal flourishing.

Figure 1.1 The building blocks of character (Jubilee Centre, 2017: 5)

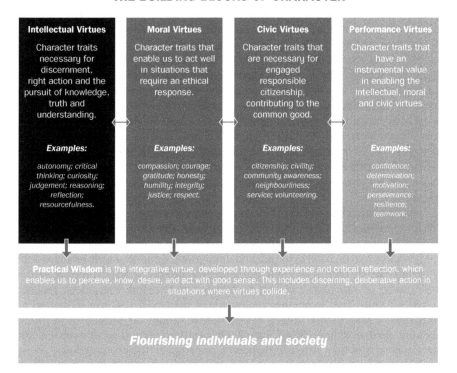

THE BUILDING BLOCKS OF CHARACTER

Intellectual Virtues	Moral Virtues	Civic Virtues	Performance Virtues
Character traits necessary for discernment, right action and the pursuit of knowledge, truth and understanding.	Character traits that enable us to act well in situations that require an ethical response.	Character traits that are necessary for engaged responsible citizenship, contributing to the common good.	Character traits that have an instrumental value in enabling the intellectual, moral and civic virtues
Examples:	*Examples:*	*Examples:*	*Examples:*
autonomy; critical thinking; curiosity; judgement; reasoning; reflection; resourcefulness.	*compassion; courage; gratitude; honesty; humility; integrity; justice; respect.*	*citizenship; civility; community awareness; neighbourliness; service; volunteering.*	*confidence; determination; motivation; perseverance; resilience; teamwork.*

Practical Wisdom is the integrative virtue, developed through experience and critical reflection, which enables us to perceive, know, desire, and act with good sense. This includes discerning, deliberative action in situations where virtues collide.

Flourishing individuals and society

Earlier in this chapter we also mentioned that a wide range of virtues are used in and across schools focusing on character education. There is no single or definitive list of such virtues – or indeed of their definitions. However, in Table 1.2 we present an indicative list of virtues and their basic definitions – separated into the four types in the building blocks model – that in our experience are commonly focused on in schools that adopt an explicit character education approach.

While schools taking an intentional and explicit approach to character education seek typically to foster a range of virtues, they will often place a core set of virtues at the heart of their work. Most often this consists of a set of three to five virtues, but some schools choose a wider set of 10 or even 12 virtues, or seek to expand their initial set of virtues once these have been successfully embedded within the school. In these schools, the language of character is foundational in, and to, their work.

The language of character

All schools and other education settings have a set of values that guide their work. In those schools that approach pupils' personal and social development through character, these values are cast as character virtues or character strengths. On first reading, the distinction between values and virtues may seem pedantic or something to concern academic philosophers more than teachers in schools. While values and virtues can sit alongside each other in the vision and mission of schools, their difference is, however, important. Generally speaking, a value is a principle or goal that we believe is important, whether to ourselves, to an organisation (such as a school), or to a community. A virtue, as we have suggested above, is a intrinsically worthwhile quality. On the other hand, any subjectively chosen preference can count as something one values; for example, one can value a strong cup of tea or a starry night. Virtues also say something much deeper about the person who possesses them, and this can be illustrated with a simple example. There is a notable difference in emphasis between the statement 'my friend values honesty' and the statement 'my friend has the virtue of honesty'. The first statement tells us that the friend thinks and believes honesty is important, whereas the second tells us something of the character of the friend and the kind of friend they are (in this case, an honest friend).

Using an explicit language of character and virtues in schools is also important for a number of related reasons. As we have already seen, the language of personal and moral development is not necessarily straightforward; terms are complex and can be used in vague and ambiguous ways. A simple example can illustrate this further. It is commonplace now in education to talk about the importance of teaching children to respect others. But what does respect actually mean? Two academic philosophers may well disagree about what constitutes respect, disagreeing about how it should be defined. Now think about a child in school. They have their own understanding of respect, but having been told by a teacher to show 'more respect' they are confused when

Table 1.2 Example virtues by type with basic definitions

Moral virtues	Intellectual virtues	Civic virtues	Performance virtues
Compassion – showing care and concern for someone who is suffering	Curiosity – being eager to know or learn something new	Citizenship – being an active, involved member of communities	Determination – commitment to completing a specific task, particularly when challenging
Courage – acting with bravery in fearful situations	Critical thinking – thinking reflectively, questioning, and arriving at independent conclusions	Civility – engaging with others with kind, courteous, and respectful conduct	Teamwork – ability to work with others effectively
Honesty – telling the truth and being sincere	Creativity – using imagination to create new ideas, insights, and items	Community awareness – actively learning from, and sharing information with, different parts of the community	Perseverance – consistent commitment to a task or action over a longer term, particularly when faced with difficulties
Justice – understanding and upholding what is right	Open-mindedness – willing to consider and discuss new ideas	Service – a commitment to working with and for others	Leadership – helping and supporting others to do the right thing by setting a vision and example
Gratitude – feeling appreciation towards someone or something	Reflection – considering alternative possibilities and not jumping to conclusions	Neighbourliness – being friendly and helpful to those nearby	Confidence – being sure about yourself, about your abilities, and about the best course of action

the teacher's definition of what respect means differs from their own. By using an explicit vocabulary of character and virtues, meanings become clarified and more consistent, offering the possibility that members of the school community – pupils, teachers, other staff, governors, parents, and others involved in the life of the school – can develop a shared understanding. As pupils become more familiar with the language, they can reflect critically on these meanings.

Key principles of effective practice in character education

Despite a significant growth of research in the field over the last two decades, there remains a need for more research on what effective practice in character education consists of. That said, a number of research-informed frameworks and syntheses of research provide a set of key principles to guide the systematic implementation of character education in schools (Lucas, 2019). In Table 1.3 we set out four examples of these key principles.

Table 1.3   Key principles of effective practice in character education

---

The Jubilee Centre for Character and Virtues' Key Principles for Character Education (2017: 3)

- 'Character is educable and its progress can be assessed holistically
- Character is important: it contributes to human and societal flourishing
- Good education is good character education
- Character is largely caught through role-modelling and emotional contagion: school culture and ethos are therefore central
- A school culture that enables students to satisfy their needs for positive relationships, competence, and self-determination facilitates the acquisition of good character
- Character should also be taught: direct teaching of character provides the rationale, language and tools to use in developing character elsewhere in and out of school
- Character should be developed in partnership with parents, employers and other community organisations
- Character education is about fairness and each child has a right to character development
- Positive character development empowers students and is liberating
- Good character demonstrates a readiness to learn from others
- Good character promotes democratic citizenship and autonomous decision-making'

Character.org's 11 Principles Framework (https://www.character.org/11-principles-framework)

- 'Core values are defined, implemented, and embedded into school culture
- The school defines "character" comprehensively to include thinking, feeling, and doing

---

(continued)

Table 1.3   (*continued*)

- The school uses a comprehensive, intentional, and proactive approach to develop character
- The school creates a caring community
- The school provides students with opportunities for moral action
- The school offers a meaningful and challenging academic curriculum that respects all learners, develops their character, and helps them to succeed
- The school fosters students' self-motivation
- All staff share the responsibility for developing, implementing, and modeling ethical character
- The school's character initiative has shared leadership and long-range support for continuous improvement
- The school engages families and community as partners in the character initiative
- The school assesses its implementation of character education, its culture and climate, and the character growth of students on a regular basis'

Berkowitz, Bier and McCauley's PRIMED model (2017: 38; see also, Berkowitz, 2021)

- '**P**rioritization: prioritization of character and social emotional development in school
- **R**elationships: strategic and intentional promotion of healthy relationships among all school stakeholders
- **I**ntrinsic motivation: promotion of the internalisation of core values/virtues through intrinsic motivational strategies
- **M**odeling: all adults and older students model core values/virtues and social-emotional competencies
- **E**mpowerment: schools empower all stakeholders as co-owners and co-authors of the character education initiative and the school in general
- **D**evelopmental pedagogy: schools intentionally foster the development of student character and socio-emotional competence and utilise methods that are developmental in purpose'

McGrath's Prototype of Character Education – 7 Key Features (2018: 26)

- '[It] is school based
- is structured
- addresses specific positive psychological attributes
- addresses identity
- addresses moral growth
- addresses holistic growth
- addresses the development of practical wisdom'

> **Reflective Activity 1.3: What do these principles have in common?**
>
> Looking at the sets of key principles in Table 1.3, identify which principles are common to all four lists. Which principles do you think it would be most important to prioritise for a school seeking to adopt a character-based approach to pupils' personal and social development? Can you find any other frameworks and/or sets of principles to add to the four in the table here?

The development and evaluation of character

If teachers wish to develop the character of pupils, they need to think about how character develops. A not inconsiderable amount of educational practice is grounded in the idea that children (and we might extend this into adolescence and early adulthood) develop through a series of stages. Two prominent examples of this kind of thinking are Jean Piaget's theory of cognitive development and Lawrence Kohlberg's (1987) theory of moral development. Most advocates of character education take a different approach. They understand that rather than being a gradual process through set stages of development, character develops in multiple, more complex ways. In addition, the cultivation and refinement of character for most – if not all – is a lifelong process. In other words, character is in constant development and is subject to a range of formative processes from early upbringing, through early years education, primary schooling, the developing importance of peers, secondary schooling, puberty, adolescence, and so on. And, of course, for some these formative processes are more supportive in developing positive forms of character than for others. There are a number of theoretical accounts that lay out what an Aristotelian-inspired account of moral development would look like (Jubilee Centre, 2017; Kristjánsson, 2015; Sanderse, 2015). These include ideas about how people can move, for example, from a lack of self-control to self-control to full virtue. They also say something more generally about the relationship between development and age; for example, that young children typically learn character through habituation and close role-models and that emphasis on practical wisdom grows as children age (although Aristotle wrote notably little about how practical wisdom could be taught).

In practice, and much like life itself, the formation of character in childhood is usually full of twists and turns! For teachers, this can be a challenging thought. However, there are several key messages that teachers can, and should, hold on to; namely, that:

> character educators should never give up hope that an individual student can be helped on the way to full autonomous virtue. No two people will progress towards virtue in exactly the same way, nor at exactly the same speed. All provisions in the field of character education thus need to take account of contextual and individual differences and seek practical solutions that work for each individual school, class or student. (Jubilee Centre, 2017: 3)

The thorny question of how character develops raises associated questions about how character education in schools can be assessed and evaluated. Clearly, careful and thoughtful assessment and evaluation forms an important part of character education in any school. As was shown in Table 1.3, one of Character.org's 11 Principles is that 'the school assesses its implementation of character education, its culture and climate, and the character growth of students on a regular basis'.[5] Rather than having a separate chapter on the measurement, assessment, and evaluation of character, in this book we opt to make some general comments here and then; like other aspects of character education introduced to you in this chapter, we return to these with a more practical focus at relevant points in the chapters that follow.

No account of assessment and evaluation of character education in today's educational landscape should fail to mention the dominant role of tests and assessments within the wider culture of schooling and education systems. Children today face a life of tests and assessments. Should these be added to by assessing character? There is no straightforward answer to this question, and schools and teachers have to make their own decisions about what is most appropriate in their contexts. In guiding these decisions, certain considerations are paramount. Perhaps the foremost of these considerations is the need to be clear as to the precise focus and rationale for any assessment and evaluation of character. Given the complexity of character, it is very difficult to measure the holistic 'character' of an individual whether at a particular moment or over a given period of time. It is, however, appropriate for teachers to measure changes in one or several virtues to gauge the effectiveness of particular interventions or to assess for formative purposes the development of one or more components of virtue. In doing so, a range of carefully planned data should be drawn upon, including pupils' self-reports/self-measures, and other evidence such as teacher reports, observations, and written reflections to produce a more rounded picture.

A second consideration is that schools should certainly seek to *evaluate* their character education in ways other than focusing on the effectiveness of specific interventions. Schools may, for instance, work to build up a body of evidence from a range of sources and stakeholders (pupils, staff, families, governors, members of the local community) about how their culture and ethos contributes to the development of pupils' character. Additionally, schools might ask pupils to evaluate – or more accurately self-evaluate – their own character (Jubilee Centre, 2017). When conducted appropriately, and when supported by teachers and other educators, asking pupils to reflect on their character and to consider their strengths and areas for development can be a powerful exercise. The Jubilee Centre for Character and Virtues' *Character Education Evaluation Handbook for Schools* (Harrison et al., 2016a: 17–18) provides advice on the evaluation of character education in and by schools. The advice given includes the following:

- *Undertake formative not summative evaluation*: Evaluation should be undertaken for educational purposes to support the building of character in children and young people. It should not be undertaken to give them character grades.

- *Value and understand the importance of professional judgements*: The professional judgements of teachers are crucial to successful evaluation.
- *Use mixed methods to triangulate the evidence to get the fullest possible picture*: To gain the best picture of character and character education, multiple sources of evidence should be drawn upon.
- *Use multiple voices in the evaluation*: Where possible, as many people in the school community should have a 'voice' in the evaluation.
- *Recognise and acknowledge the limitations of evaluating character.*

Finally, though not strictly a form of assessment or evaluation, schools will often seek to *recognise* character. Recognising character often takes the form of character report cards and awards. Whether focusing on character as a whole or on specific virtues, through report cards and awards the conduct and action of pupils can be recognised and celebrated. As we have said already, however, the use of character report cards to recognise character must both draw on and form part of a wider approach to assessing and evaluating character within the school. In Fig. 1.2 we identify some possible tools and forms of assessment and evaluation relevant to character education (for those who want to delve deeper into questions surrounding the evaluation of character, we recommend the recent book by Wright et al., 2021; see also Curren and Kotzee, 2014; Hanson et al., 2012; Urban and Trochim, 2017).

Figure 1.2 Assessment and evaluation of character education

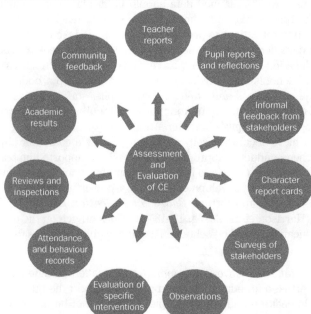

Conclusion

In this chapter, you have been introduced to many of the core elements of character education, including how character education relates to the closely related fields of positive education and social and emotional learning. To summarise the key points made in this chapter:

- Character consists a set of personal qualities – or virtues – that are morally worthwhile and that enable us to live productive, socially engaged, and, as an ultimate aim, flourishing lives.
- Character education is the deliberate and intentional cultivation of virtues, including the meta-virtue of practical wisdom, within schools.
- Character education is closely linked to other educational approaches to pupils' personal and social development, most notably positive education and social and emotional learning. While these approaches overlap, they are not identical – though in practice schools will often combine approaches.
- Various frameworks and sets of key principles are available to guide the work of schools, and together these emphasise certain essential processes.
- Core elements of character education include the building blocks of character and the language of character.
- Because of the complex and ever-evolving nature of pupils' character, schools and teachers need to take a cautious and considered approach to both how character develops and how character can be evaluated.

As you work through the chapters in this book you will be introduced to various ideas, research findings, and practical examples that shed more light on, and examine in more detail, these ideas. To stimulate the application of your initial thinking about character education, we finish this chapter with three case studies. In these case studies, you will see how the points summarised above come together within the work of Colmore Junior School in England, Regent International School in Dubai, and Great Hearts Academies in the United States. As you read through them, you will see how some of the core ideas examined in this chapter play out in school settings, both explicitly and implicitly. As a collective, the three case studies also highlight further elements of character education that we explore in detail in the chapters that follow.

Case Study 1.1: The 7 Key Principles at Colmore Junior School

ROBIN VENN, Teacher and Character Education Lead, Colmore Junior School, Birmingham, UK

In 2017, our school began to prepare and rationalise our character education meaning and provision across pupils, staff, and the wider community. Some of this was done in preparation for the arrival of the non-statutory DfE *Character Education Framework Guidance* that was due in 2019. There was, however, more than a new set of political guidelines that motivated our thoughts. We needed to understand what character education meant for our pupils and the positive impact that it could have on their lives and time at school.

The headteacher, myself, and the teacher responsible for Citizenship worked together to understand what 'character education' was at Colmore and how we could make it more explicit, including through a more formal approach. One of the first interesting pieces of research that we carried out was to survey the parents and ask them what skills and qualities they wanted their children to leave with. The answers were overwhelmingly in favour of leadership, independence, happiness, and resilience. Parents deemed these the important qualities to develop that would help their children in life, regardless of academic achievement.

The second part of research we carried out was to survey the staff and to begin some discussion and debate. This was achieved through a set of formal continuing professional development sessions guided by the headteacher. Again this proved interesting for different reasons. Some teachers quite rightly believed that they were already teaching 'character education' and that there was no need to be more explicit, while some were unaware of the meaning outside of Religious Education (RE) or Personal, Social, Health, and Economic (PSHE) education. This was our first step in defining our offering and in introducing a caught, taught, and sought approach. It became important to us to help teachers understand that character education was much more than teachers responding to moral dilemmas in the classroom and more than delivering prescribed and compulsory lessons in RE or PSHE. It had to be a whole-school approach that involved many of the aspects of daily life and the formation of a common language that the children could identify with and practise.

Engaging in professional development on character education helped us to understand what was meant by a caught, taught, and sought approach and how we might implement character across our school. It was important for us to remember that we were trying to adapt the culture of the school by helping the teachers understand the depth and meaning of the moral and virtuous impact they have as role models to pupils.

The headteacher played a pivotal role in the development of the new structure, providing the space and time for us to think about character education and supporting us in embedding new ideas and material. After some months of planning and deliberation, we arrived at our '7 Key Principles'. These were to be the foundation of character education at Colmore:

- Leadership
- Resilience
- Independence
- Globally and Locally Aware
- Creativity
- Inclusivity
- Healthy and Well.

An important part of our approach involves helping pupils to recognise and understand character education opportunities around them. Pupils joining our school in Year 3 are introduced to the 7 Key Principles and are given opportunities to develop their language around them. Teachers point out opportunities for pupils, explaining how they relate to the principles. Opportunities are spotted in advance by teachers during their weekly planning, preparation, and assessment (PPA) time and are planned moments. They can be in any subject and for any principle.

Pupils who display their grasp of the principles are awarded a postcard to take home and celebrate with their family. We designed this as a way to keep the pupils and our wider community engaged with the principles. Each time a pupil earns a postcard, the teacher records it on a whole-school register that stays with the pupil as they progress through our school. By the time the pupils are in Year 5 or 6, they would be expected to have earned all of the principles and are then awarded a 'principle' badge for their uniform. We have found that the badges provide extra motivation for pupils to explore each of the school's principles.

Our journey is certainly not complete yet and will continue to evolve. We are constantly looking at ways to improve and adapt our character education provision and to provide our pupils with opportunities to flourish.

Case Study 1.2: Positive Education and Character at Regent International School

Dr Kayleigh Sumner, Educational Psychologist, Head of Positive Education and Wellbeing, Fortes Education, Dubai, United Arab Emirates

Our character education journey began in 2011 when we launched our Education in Human Values programme with a focus on 5 Core Virtues: truth, love, right conduct, non-violence, and peace. As our school has expanded, character education has remained central to our core purpose, which over time has evolved into our Positive Education curriculum and ethos in 2016.

Positive education is the whole-school wellbeing approach that we use and is underpinned by the key principles of positive psychology. It combines learning with resilience, building character, and enhancing wellbeing. We use Seligman's (2011) PERMA model as a framework for our practice, enriched with the focus on health. At Fortes Schools we have six pillars of the PERMA+H framework that includes Positive Emotions, Engagement, Relationships, Meaning, Accomplishment, and Health. The framework is designed to promote flourishing and is underpinned by a set of 24 character strengths.

We adopted a whole-school approach and launched the programme alongside the Institute of Positive Education. All of our staff participate in a three-day positive education induction programme and have access to ongoing training throughout the year. To ensure positive education is applied consistently and remains a priority on the agenda, we have dedicated positive education 'champions' across all key stages and specialist departments. These members of staff work as key drivers ensuring that positive education principles are weaved throughout our core subjects.

Pupils have access to weekly Values in Action (in primary school) and Science of Wellbeing (in secondary school) lessons that involve exploring one of the 24 character strengths. These lessons provide opportunities to discuss, build upon, and develop character strengths each week. We have positive education champions and wellbeing ambassadors throughout the school who work on projects that feed into our wider strategic vision. Pupils utilise specific wellbeing strategies taught through the Positive Education curriculum to support them to build resilience and healthy coping strategies, including resilient thinking, developing problem-solving skills, using strengths, and expressing gratitude.

To ensure we reach the whole school community, parents are offered monthly positive education workshops where they learn about resilience, growth mindset, and character strengths spotting. Parents have the opportunity to come into school to see positive education in action. We work on joint projects with the parent governors to empower the wider community and share the principles of positive education.

We believe that our positive education priorities are based on the unique context of our school in Dubai, thus an essential aspect of our approach involves auditing, measuring, and evaluating the processes and impact of positive education in school. We regularly disseminate bespoke surveys to staff, children, and parents to measure wellbeing and identify areas of development to feed into our wider strategic vision. Identified areas of strength and development are weaved into phase priorities across each key stage.

Our annual wellbeing assessments have suggested that the implementation of the positive education approach has improved the wellbeing of our pupils. This has been demonstrated through some of our key wellbeing indicators, such as ability to manage anxiety, increased sense of connectedness to others, feeling a sense of belonging to the school, and pupils' overall rating for happiness. The data we have gathered suggests that our strategic and systematic approach towards implementing positive education across the entire school community has shifted the culture of the school.

Positive education has supported us to work towards our whole-school vision in empowering pupils to access a high-quality value-based education to achieve their potential and flourish in a changing world. It has not been a quick or simple transformation, as building a positive educational community requires considerable time, dedication by school leadership, as well as commitment and passion on the part of teachers and staff. We continue to work towards systemic and curriculum enhancement to ensure we remain up to date with current research and what we do promotes a collective effort of working towards our whole-school vision and the unique context of our school.

Case Study 1.3: Great Hearts Academies: Schooling that Aspires to Greatness

ROBERT L. JACKSON, Chief Academic Officer, Great Hearts America, United States

When the first Great Hearts Academy, Veritas Preparatory, opened in Phoenix in the fall of 2002, a community of families, teachers, and staff gave public expression to an educational model drawn from traditional private schooling. The 'college prep' experience, once the privilege of tuition-paying families, was now available to the general public and subsidized by the state under charter school law.

While scores of charter schools were formed to improve academic performance in the first decade of US charter laws (Minnesota being the first in 1994), only a handful drew their educational models from perennial forms dating back to antiquity. Yet, the crest of Veritas Preparatory Academy (VPA) boldly features a book whose open pages are inscribed with '*Verum Bonum Pulchrum*' alongside '*Athenae Hierusalem Roma*'. The school's first principles – Truth, Goodness, Beauty – are thus recognized as the legacy of that distinctive multicultural civilization which emerged in the ancient Mediterranean.

The founders of VPA promoted a profound synthesis of intellectual, moral, and political virtues – a synthesis derived from that ancient civilization that influenced millions across the Roman Empire. Even after Rome's fall, those ideals and institutions continued to develop and expand throughout diverse communities, becoming an increasingly capacious civilization of intellectual and moral ideals. From an educational legacy dating back to ancient Greece, VPA unassumingly propagates the great works of philosophy, literature, history, and religion as studies worthy of emulation. In short, this six-year program of study (Grades 7–12) highlights the humanities of an integrated liberal arts curriculum, including mathematics, languages, the sciences, and fine arts – as well as competitive athletics.

Great Hearts later adopted the tagline 'Classical Education – Revolutionary Schools', emphasizing the model's time-tested sources alongside its radical potential. Within several years, one prep school had grown to a half dozen, and the parent organization, Great Hearts America, turned to elementary schools to increase the capacity to serve more pupils. The grammar grades proved to be even *more* popular with parents, creating demand that has outstripped the organization's ability to multiply. What began with 120 pupils in a rental facility in 2002 has grown to 20 campuses across three metropolitan areas (Phoenix, San Antonio, Dallas/Ft Worth) serving more than 21,000 pupils – all in less than two decades. This is the direct result of parental demand for a better form of education.

But, what makes the 'classical' approach better? Certainly there is depth to the liberal arts, with the study of languages and those authors who have given memorable expression to extraordinary thought. There is also breadth to the liberal arts, as they encompass the arts and the sciences in equal measure.

Classical education recognizes that human beings require more than the development of brain matter to be fully formed. With Aristotle and his successors, Great Hearts recognizes that intellectual and moral habits are the high-road to human excellence, the routines and practices that produce personal integrity: where mind and heart are one in pursuit of the highest ideals. In short, the classical model provides a coherent and cogent expression of what it means to be a well-formed person. It does so by introducing pupils to an ongoing conversation concerning greatness, in the company of instructors committed to the same.

Every day in classrooms across the Great Hearts organization, you will see pupils puzzling over the challenges of a mathematical proof or closely reading the lineaments of a literary work or carefully observing the phenomena of the natural world – all with the purpose of developing habits of attention to the details, empathy for our human experience, and the capacity to express thought with precision, insight, and eloquence.

Which brings us back to Veritas Prep's transcendent trio, and the core purpose which has since been adopted by all Great Hearts Academies: 'to cultivate the minds and hearts of pupils through the pursuit of Truth, Goodness, and Beauty'. While such language may seem quaint, there remains a hunger in the human soul for ideals to inspire our better angels. Classical education draws upon long-standing sources to envision a better form of schooling: a revolutionary approach that just might advance an educational renaissance.

Notes

1 A third book that has gained a good deal of traction in schools, and is sometimes included in this more narrow field within positive psychology, is Carol Dweck's *Mindset: Changing the Way You Think to Fulfil Your Potential* (2017). Dweck herself has rejected this connection.
2 https://www.ipen-network.com/about-us
3 Seligman's (2011) original PERMA model was extended to PERMAH (Norrish, 2015). See also https://ppc.sas.upenn.edu/learn-more/perma-theory-well-being-and-perma-workshops
4 https://casel.org/what-is-sel/
5 https://www.character.org/11-principles-framework

Further reading

Berkowitz, M.W. (2021) *PRIMED for Character Education: Six Design Principles for School Improvement.* New York: Routledge.
Drawing on research evidence and practice in schools, a book in which the core elements of the PRIMED framework are brought to life to give detailed and insightful accounts of character education.

Collaborative for Academic, Social and Emotional Learning (2020) *CASEL's SEL Framework: What Are the Competence Areas and Where Are They Promoted?* [Online.] Available at: https://casel.org/wp-content/uploads/2020/12/CASEL-SEL-Framework-11.2020.pdf
A leading framework of SEL that sets out the CASEL 5 – five broad, interrelated areas of competence with examples. Emphasizes the key settings that, working together, support SEL.

Curren, R. and Kotzee, B. (2014) Can virtue be measured?, *Theory and Research in Education,* 12 (3): 266–282.
A journal article which explores the question of whether virtue can be measured.

Jubilee Centre for Character and Virtues (2017) *A Framework for Character Education in Schools.* Birmingham: University of Birmingham. [Online.] Available at: https://www.jubileecentre.ac.uk/userfiles/jubileecentre/pdf/character-education/Framework%20for%20Character%20Education.pdf
A theoretically and empirically research-based framework for character education based on a neo-Aristotelian viewpoint. Sets out key definitions, the building blocks of character, components of virtues, and a neo-Aristotelian model of moral development.

Kristjánsson, K. (2015) *Aristotelian Character Education.* Abingdon: Routledge.
A book that presents a detailed and thoughtful analysis of character education from a reconstructed Aristotelian perspective. The book offers a lucid account of character education, including how a neo-Aristotelian approach differs from other approaches to character education. Balances theoretical ideas and more practical questions and concerns.

2 The character of the teacher

Introduction

When asked to think back to our own experiences of schooling, we are likely to recall our friends, those subjects we enjoyed (or didn't!), and the teachers who educated us. Although we may recount breakthrough moments in which teachers helped us to succeed academically, teachers are not necessarily remembered for their subject knowledge or ability to convey factual information – it is often the *character* of the teacher that is fondly, or contemptuously, recalled. Indeed, even when fond memories of teachers concern academic success, the character of the teacher is often implicated: the support of a caring and attentive teacher who encouraged us to persevere when the concept was initially too difficult to understand; the teacher whose creativity and enthusiasm encouraged us out of our comfort zone and to participate; the compassionate teacher who supported us when our lives brought challenges; the teacher who gave up their time at the weekend to create tailored learning materials to support our needs; the list of examples goes on.

While it is irrefutable that in most cases parents and carers are the primary educators of their children, non-parental role models such as peers, other family members, teachers, and mentors also have the potential to positively influence children's personal and social development (Bowers et al., 2014; Johnson et al., 2016). Children can and do learn more from teachers than the information conveyed in lessons. In part this is due to the amount of time teachers spend with their pupils, but it is also due to the developmental ages at which children attend school and the nature of what occurs within educational settings. Teachers ultimately play an important role in pupils' character development and construction of self-identity through the kindness and support they show the children in their care (Harrison et al., 2016c).

The work of teachers is complex and varied, incorporating a range of elements, including the communication of important moral, social, and cultural information. Most, if not all, teachers acknowledge that their personal character influences their teaching and note that personal moral values such as respect, caring, fairness, trust, and empathy influence professional practice (Joseph, 2016; Peterson and Arthur, 2021). A teacher's tone and voice often convey hidden meanings, and pupils are also sensitive to non-verbal communications; pupils make judgements about whether teachers truly care about them and their development based on cues taken from a teacher's demeanour, body language, and facial expressions.

How a teacher communicates with others, their daily interactions, and how they make decisions are all influenced by who they are as a person. The focus of this chapter is on the *character* of the teacher and the role a teacher's character plays in informing and guiding conduct. The chapter is divided into several sections. Within the first section teaching is presented as a profession which inherently contains moral and ethical dimensions. In this, the role of teachers and teachers' motivations for joining the profession are briefly discussed. The second section attends to the standards and codes of conduct that inform teachers' work. Consideration of these standards highlights how character is implicated in a teacher's professional responsibilities. In the third section, the manner, speech, and behaviour of teachers is considered, and the influence of the teacher as a role model is discussed. In the fourth section, the desirable character virtues of 'good' teachers are discussed and explained.

Chapter Objectives

By the end of this chapter, you should have:

- Considered how a teacher's character influences the pupils in their care
- Evaluated how character is incorporated within teachers' standards and codes of conduct within your own context
- Reflected on the character virtues and qualities of a 'good' teacher.

Teaching as a moral endeavour

The moral dimensions and ethical requirements of teaching are well documented and understood within education literature, which positions teaching as an overtly moral endeavour (Arthur, 2003; Carr, 2007; Cooke and Carr, 2014; Peterson and Arthur, 2021). However, it is apparent that the tendency of education reforms to prioritise academic attainment and preparation for employability in schools has led to a lack of clarity around what the role of the teacher encompasses. Due to the prioritisation of subject knowledge and technical skills within teacher preparation programmes, combined with dominant discourses around school assessment scores and the accountability of teachers and schools, teachers joining the profession would be forgiven for understanding teaching as being concerned predominantly with educating pupils for academic success. While certainly an important and focal aspect of teaching, the prioritisation of academic skills without an adequate focus on the moral dimensions and ethical requirements of teaching risks teachers losing sight of what it truly means to be a teacher and what a responsibility for pupils' *well-rounded education* encompasses to its full extent.

Education is not limited to the teaching and learning of purely technical skills or the inculcation of knowledge, and it is generally agreed that a teacher's responsibility is for the holistic education of pupils, including personal and moral development (Bullough, 2011; Campbell, 2008a; Lapsley and Woodbury, 2016; Osguthorpe, 2013; Sanger, 2012). In fact, the majority of teachers choose the profession for reasons associated with pupils' personal and social development, informed by moral or altruistic motivations (Book and Freeman, 1986; Brookhart and Freeman, 1992; Peterson and Arthur, 2021; Sanger and Osguthorpe, 2011). New entrants to the teaching profession will typically cite the desire to make a difference to children's lives (Arthur et al., 2015b; Sanger and Osguthorpe, 2013), to develop good people, to inspire, to foster a love of learning, and to attend to the welfare and development of young people as motivating reasons for becoming a teacher. In other words, it is very often the desire to support pupils' personal and social development – including their moral development – that underpins why the majority of teachers teach.

Teachers make a wide range of decisions about pupils as part of their daily work – their safety, their wellbeing, their learning, and their relationships. At all times, and sometimes in the face of other competing pressures, teachers act with the best interests of their pupils at heart. In this way, we can think of teachers as acting *in loco parentis* – in place of the parent within the context of the school. A teacher's role carries with it a high degree of public trust, and because of this teachers are considered to shoulder a higher level of moral responsibility than many other professions (Arthur et al., 2017b). Teachers are also inevitable role models for pupils whose attitudes, dispositions, and behaviours are constantly on display and under scrutiny. Accordingly, teachers are expected to uphold high standards of ethics and behaviour in both personal and professional domains. It is important to consider that the teacher's influence as an educator is not confined to the school building. A teacher's conduct and presence is often keenly observed by pupils, parents, and other school stakeholders outside of the school, including in online spaces and through social media. The character of the teacher – who they truly are as a person – is a central concern in teaching. In the words of Arthur et al. (2017b: 6), 'the act of teaching ... reveals the centrality of a teacher's moral and intellectual character' and the public have a vested interest in this.

It is also important to consider the moral dimensions of interactions and relationships between teachers and pupils. Typically, a child's first and most consistent source of moral and ethical guidance comes from the home (Jubilee Centre, 2017; Peterson and Arthur, 2021). However, teachers also share in this responsibility. Pupils spend a considerable amount of time in the presence and care of teachers and, as will be explored later in this chapter, teachers are likely to influence pupils not only as potential role models, but as exemplars of good conduct and behaviour who set standards and expectations through their daily interactions with pupils. Teachers can motivate or discourage, can inspire or deflate, and can teach pupils a great deal through what they encourage or discourage within the school and classroom environments. This form of teaching is considered to be an implicit form of moral education which occurs whether acknowledged by teachers or not (Arthur et al., 2017b).

Due to the moral nature of teaching, and because teachers work so closely with pupils, parents, and other educators, teachers are regularly faced with complex situations that have moral dimensions and require action to be taken. In such situations, the 'right thing' to do is not clear cut and it can be said that a teacher faces a moral dilemma. In being tasked with navigating moral dilemmas in their daily practice, teachers are in a constant process of judgement and arbitration (Fullard and Watts, 2019), and rely on practical wisdom to guide them. As outlined in Chapter 1, practical wisdom develops through experience and habituation, and it is ultimately the character of the teacher which guides their choices and actions when faced with a moral dilemma.

Despite the moral nature of teaching and the understanding that teachers contribute to pupils' personal and social development, in recent years the moral dimensions of teaching have not always received the attention they should within teacher preparation and early career development programmes. Guided predominantly by teachers' standards and codes of conduct – and perhaps the assumption that those entering the profession are the 'right kind of people' and therefore already have the necessary attributes – teacher preparation programmes have tended to prioritise teaching skills and competencies over more fundamental questions of character development and professionalism. However, with changes in policy, guidance, and indeed in wider society, teacher preparation programmes are paying more attention to questions of character, judgement, and professionalism. Case Study 2.1 highlights how some teacher educators have made a focus on character a conscious and significant part of teacher training and development.

Case Study 2.1: Pre-Service Teacher Education at the University of Warwick

JULIE TAYLOR, Primary and Early Years School Direct Programme Lead, Senior Teaching Fellow Centre for Teacher Education, University of Warwick, UK

At the Centre for Teacher Education at the University of Warwick, we have character and values embedded throughout our teacher education programmes. We explicitly teach about character education to help equip our student teachers to develop and instil character and moral values in the pupils they teach. However, we also recognise and prioritise the importance of the student teachers' own character and virtue development. A recent review of our Initial Teacher Education curriculum and our departmental vision and values allowed for the implementation of a number of planned and purposeful opportunities throughout our one-year Post-Graduate Certificate of Education programmes to explore and develop the character of the teacher.

One strand that has had a positive impact on student teacher character development is our work on professionalism. Teaching is a particularly challenging profession, as it is fraught with complexities, and teachers face ethical dilemmas on a daily basis that lack a clear resolution. Without support in the development of practical wisdom, early career teachers may not feel sufficiently prepared to know how to best respond when faced with challenging situations. Therefore, our department has deliberately moved away from the traditional approach to professionalism that focuses on adherence to professional codes of conduct, as this fails to prepare student teachers for the reality of teaching. Instead, we revisit professionalism through workshop-style seminars built around ethical dilemmas to guide student teachers to consider what it means to be a professional and to understand more fully the ensuing moral responsibilities and challenges that come with being a teacher. With personal tutors facilitating the exploration of authentic professional dilemmas, student teachers are able to openly discuss how they might respond to a particular situation collaboratively and in a safe space to consider the most appropriate course of action. This process has proved to be effective in equipping student teachers to more confidently deal with issues that arise on their professional placements.

The concept of professional identity is revisited at key reflection points during the year in the student teachers' e-portfolios to capture their evolving professional identity. For example, during induction, student teachers have the opportunity to reflect on the character of teachers that have inspired them in their own education and the values they hope to embody as a teacher. Student teachers are invested in this process as the majority want to become a teacher for altruistic reasons. By providing opportunities to reflect on the kind of teacher student teachers aspire to be throughout, we help them to maintain a sense of purpose and the motivation needed to enable them to cope with the challenges and demands of the pre-service year.

We tend to find that student teachers have had little opportunity for self-reflection prior to commencing their teacher preparation programme. As a result, many begin without having developed the self-awareness to recognise their own character strengths and areas for development. With research indicating that teachers are viewed as role models by their pupils and that character can be both caught and taught, teacher educators at Warwick believe that it is part of our responsibility to support student teachers to develop critical reflection skills and nurture a commitment to their own personal growth to support and complement their development as effective classroom practitioners. To ensure that we address this responsibility, we have built in regular opportunities for guided reflection on character through both the individual tutorial programme and designated reflection sessions at key points throughout the year. To support reflection while the student teachers are on their school placements, we developed a framework aligning our Core Warwick Values of Social Justice, Intellectual Curiosity and Creativity with the virtue building blocks from the Jubilee Centre for Character and Virtues' *A Framework for Character Education in Schools* (2017), and included a glossary of definitions to ensure consistent understanding of the values.

While on school placements, student teachers are supported in a number of ways. During their weekly meetings with mentors, student teachers have coaching conversations about their developing classroom practice. They are also encouraged to use the framework as a guide to enable them to reflect on their own values. This may include identifying which values have been particularly significant that week, values they feel they have made progress with, and recognising which values may need further development. To support student teachers who may initially struggle with this process, mentors are also encouraged to provide feedback on character development as part of this regular professional dialogue. Mentors themselves are also encouraged to self-reflect on their own values through our mentor development programmes. We advocate an ethical coaching model which moves away from the traditional hierarchical model that is so prevalent in traditional mentoring relationships. Where mentors are prepared to devote time to self-reflection, they recognise the impact their character has on their mentees and adapt their mentoring style accordingly, thus personalising their approach to most effectively meet the needs of the individual trainee.

Character, teachers' standards, codes of conduct, and professional responsibilities

At this point in the chapter, it is necessary to consider how the concept of character connects with a teacher's professional role and responsibilities, as set out by government and non-governmental bodies in various forms of teachers' standards and codes of conduct. The standards that teachers work towards and within will be familiar to any pre-service student teacher. These standards are often a primary focus in the training and development of all teachers, with conduct and practice evidenced in line with the standards. Once qualified, standards for teachers remain important, but these can often sit more in the background than for beginning teachers. In Australia, for example, the Australian Institute for Teaching and School Leadership (AITSL) has set out professional standards which frame development in each standard according to career stage and professional capability: 'Graduate', 'Proficient', 'Highly Accomplished', or 'Lead'. At the 'Graduate' level of standard 7, in which teachers 'meet professional ethics and responsibilities', teachers are expected to 'understand and apply the key principles described in codes of ethics and conduct for the teaching profession'. At the highest level ('Lead'), teachers 'model exemplary ethical behaviour and exercise informed judgements in all professional dealings with students, colleagues and the community' (AITSL, 2018: 22).

In most, if not all, educational jurisdictions, standards for teachers will include a similar ethical dimension focused on the character of the teacher. However, teachers' standards commonly face criticism for focusing too much on technical competency and not enough on the character and qualities that teachers should demonstrate (Beauchamp et al., 2015; Fullard and Watts, 2019). In England, the *Teachers' Standards* (DfE, 2013) focus largely on skills, echoing a technicist model of teaching. Typically, standards for teachers emphasise criteria which are focused on a teacher's level of knowledge and professional responsibilities. It has been argued that standards such as these lack a framework of values and qualities conducive to the profession, focusing too much on what teachers *do* and not enough on what a teacher *is* (Arthur et al., 2005).

However, despite a general lack of emphasis on the character and qualities that teachers should demonstrate, the character of the teacher is undoubtedly implicated in their personal and professional conduct. Having introduced the different categories (or building blocks) of character virtues in Chapter 1, it will be possible for readers to unpick some of the more generic statements and mechanical language in different versions of teachers' standards and codes of conduct, and to highlight how a teacher's character, if not explicitly mentioned, is implicated in these. Take, for example, the first statement in Box 2.1. It only takes a few seconds to tease out the desirable character virtues that underpin this statement: namely, that teachers must be *honest*, *kind*, *respectful*, and *helpful* (to name only a few).

Reflective Activity 2.1: Identifying implicit character virtues

Consider the statements provided in Box 2.1. Which character virtues would you expect teachers to have and demonstrate in order to satisfy these statements? You might find it helpful to refer back to Table 1.2 for a list of different virtues.

Box 2.1: Statements taken from the *Teachers' Standards* in England (DfE, 2013)

Teachers **must**:

1 'demonstrate consistently the positive attitudes, values and behaviour which are expected of pupils' (2013: 10)
2 'maintain good relationships with pupils, exercise appropriate authority, and act decisively when necessary' (2013: 12)
3 'uphold public trust in the profession and maintain high standards of ethics and behaviour, within and outside school, by:
   • treating pupils with dignity, building relationships rooted in mutual respect' (2013: 14)

In other parts of the UK, standards for teachers arguably pay more attention to character and are less ambiguous in their wording than in England. One need only look at the first few pages of the draft *Professional Standards for Teachers in Scotland* (GTCS, 2021) to see explicit mention of the character virtues that teachers must demonstrate: *trust*, *respect*, *honesty*, *courage*, *wisdom*, *truthfulness*, and *integrity*. Furthermore, the teacher's role in contributing to a 'caring and compassionate ethos' (GTCS, 2021: 5) is emphasised. In Wales, the *Code of Professional Conduct and Practice* (EWC, 2019: 3) makes explicit teachers' 'personal responsibility as a role model', acknowledging the influence of teachers who will be admired and emulated; and in Northern Ireland, the *Professional Standards for Teachers* (LLUK, 2009) outlines six professional values for teachers, including empathy and trust, respect, and creativity.

Reflective Activity 2.2: Evaluating the teachers' standards or codes of conduct in your own educational context

In this activity, you are asked to evaluate the standards or codes of conduct set for teachers in your own educational jurisdiction. To do this, you will first need to access and read through the relevant document(s), which are usually accessible on government websites and may be provided during teacher training. Next, you will need to evaluate how, and the extent to which, the character of the teacher is implicated. To do this, you might ask the following questions when reviewing the document(s):

- Which moral, intellectual, civic, and performance virtues are mentioned explicitly within the standards?
- Which virtues are implicit, or implicated in the standards?
- To what extent do the standards focus on technical competencies and how does this compare to a focus on the teacher's character?
- Do the standards make reference to professional judgement?
- Which virtues are missing, in your opinion?

Finally, suggest changes that could be made to the standards or codes of conduct so that they include a more explicit focus on the character of the teacher – you might like to make changes directly onto the document in a different colour, or to re-write certain statements. You should be able to explain why you have made these changes and why you think they are relevant to the profession.

A teacher's influence on pupils as a role model

Whether teachers acknowledge their role as an exemplar or not, young people in their care will learn from their manner, behaviour, attitudes and dispositions.
– Sandra Cooke, 2017: 420

In the early parts of this chapter we argued that beyond the teaching of subject knowledge and transferrable skills, there is a certain inevitability of teachers influencing pupils' character development as positive role models and mentors in schools; teachers are always 'on display' as exemplars of speech, behaviour, and general conduct. As Cooke notes in the quotation above, regardless of whether teachers are aware of their influence or not, teachers influence pupils through their very presence and behaviours. Various research studies suggest that how teachers enact their wider responsibilities for pupils' personal and social development is ultimately perceived to depend on a teacher's character and presence (Fenstermacher et al., 2009; Peterson and Arthur, 2021; Richardson and Fallona, 2001; Tickle, 2001).

There is a common perception within the field of character education that teachers are role models for the pupils in their care (Arthur et al., 2017b; Harrison et al., 2016c; Lumpkin, 2008; Osguthorpe, 2008; Revell and Arthur, 2007; Sanderse, 2013). This view is also shared by the Department for Education (DfE) in England, which outlines the following guidance for the preparation of teachers in the *Initial Teacher Training (ITT): Core Content Framework* (DfE, 2019b: 9): 'Teachers are key role models, who can influence the attitudes, values and behaviours of their students'. This guidance clearly acknowledges the powerful influence of teachers on their pupils. Student teachers and qualified teachers also share in in this view, often acknowledging that modelling is one of the primary means through which they can influence the moral development of their pupils (Arthur et al., 2015c; Sanger and Osguthorpe, 2013). Accordingly, Harrison et al. (2016c) assert that teachers must accept responsibility as role models, and set examples of appropriate behaviours in different situations.

Attention paid to role models in education has often focused on the *imitation* or *emulation* of individuals. In this way, role-modelling is sometimes understood as little more than holding up individuals as those worthy of emulation in the hope that the individual's 'worth' will become apparent to pupils and that, in turn, pupils will seek to imitate these positive attitudes and behaviours. For Kristjánsson (2006b: 46), this view of role-model education, which emphasises behavioural elements, is 'to a large extent, educationally under-ambitious and morally under-developed'. Instead, Kristjánsson advocates an alternative form of role-model education which accounts for affective, conative, cognitive, and behavioural elements. In other words, a form of role-model education in which pupils are able to identify the qualities demonstrated by the individual, understand why the qualities are valuable, and are motivated and strive to develop these qualities themselves. In other words, a more critical and personally relevant way of learning from role models. Sanderse (2013) echoes this view and suggests that, for role-modelling to be effective, teachers need to explain not only how the exemplified qualities are morally significant for pupils, but how pupils can develop the qualities themselves.

While a focus on role models is common within literature on character education (and we return to this later in the book), teachers themselves tend to function as role models for pupils implicitly, and explicit role-modelling on the part of the teacher is likely to be employed less (Sanderse, 2013). Of course, teachers may well explicitly model good behaviour when they feel this is necessary, especially with younger children. For example, a teacher may draw attention to how they exercise virtues such as civility and kindness in speech and conduct, or how they would help and share with others. However, more often than not a teacher's influence as a role model occurs subconsciously, operating through their conduct in their interactions with pupils, colleagues, families, and community partners.

When school-aged pupils are asked to identify their character role models, described as someone who is 'looked up to' as a 'good person', parents and other familial adults are identified far more frequently than teachers (Johnson et al., 2016). Yet it is notable from the research literature that this perception changes with age. Teachers are recognised as role models to a greater extent in retrospect (Sanderse, 2013); accordingly, older pupils are far more likely than younger pupils to perceive teachers in this way (see Johnson et al., 2016), and this suggests that as pupils mature they may be more able to reflect on and identify the individuals – including teachers – who have influenced them. Younger children may understandably be less able to identify individuals who are positive (and negative) influences – be it peers, teachers, parents, siblings, or celebrities in the media – but as adolescents and adults, pupils may be more able to look back and identify not only who, but *how* individuals, such as teachers, influenced them during their formative years. It is interesting to note, too, that a large proportion of role models are chosen based on their personal qualities and characteristics which are regarded as 'character-relevant' in nature – for example, the role models are 'kind', 'caring', 'nice', and 'trustworthy' (Johnson et al., 2016).

Reflective Activity 2.3: Which teachers were role models for you?

Think about your own experiences of education and schooling. Which teachers do you remember? Do you remember individual teachers because they acted as a positive role model or because they were a negative role model (or perhaps they were a mix of both)? What did and have you learned from these teachers? Thinking back to the four types of character – moral, intellectual, civic, and performance – what virtues do you wish to 'model' for pupils?

How teachers influence pupils as role models is complex and involves a range of factors. Some pupils might identify a teacher (or teachers) as a character role model and consciously seek to emulate their manner and actions. However, as the research mentioned above suggests, the majority of pupils will not recognise fully the influence of their teachers until later in life. Some of the ways that teachers can positively influence pupils as role models are shown in Box 2.2 below, but of course there are many factors at play which may affect the strength of the influence in each case. The amount of time spent in the presence of influential models is one; teachers are more likely to be seen as positive character role models where they have formed meaningful relationships with pupils within which they demonstrate certain qualities (being kind, compassionate, honest, and so forth) in a stable and consistent manner. A teacher who spends extended periods of time with pupils may play a more significant role than a teacher who sees pupils once a week, or indirectly in and around the school. This said, it is also the case that in some instances a seminal moment in a pupil's life may be more fleeting – a momentary and unexpected act of caring or kindness is a case in point. It is important, therefore, not to underestimate the impact of even the briefest of interactions with pupils.

A teacher's character is constantly on display and is the subject of consistent evaluation. Teachers 'are under the close examination of students, who see and hear in teachers' eyes, voice and body language what they are really saying' (Arthur et al., 2017b: 8). Take a secondary school or subject-specific teacher who has limited contact time with pupils. The teacher has multiple classes a day and their time with any one pupil is limited to one hour once a week. One might question how this teacher could influence the pupils they teach beyond the academic boundaries of the classroom context. Once again, it is important to highlight that pupils' interest and engagement in a lesson is not purely down to the subject matter or a teacher's ability to convey information; pupils may well look forward (or indeed not look forward!) to even brief interactions with teachers based on *who* the teacher is and how they interact with pupils. These interactions are shaped by a teacher's conduct.

To illustrate and delve further into the influence of teachers in this way, let us consider two examples: the first, a teacher who embodies in speech and behaviour what we would generally consider to be 'good' character – someone who is kind, attentive, and respectful. When approached by a distressed pupil in a lesson or after school, the teacher makes time to speak and listen to the pupil's worries and concerns. The teacher prioritises the pupil's welfare over their other immediate responsibilities and is visibly interested in what the pupil has to say. The teacher takes time to listen, reassures the pupil, and advises them. Through the teacher's interaction, they display kindness, respect, and compassion to the pupil. This conduct enables the pupil to trust the teacher. The second is an example of a teacher who, as a result of their preoccupation with teaching knowledge and understanding, is abrupt with pupils and often displays a lack of interest in their thoughts, interests, and concerns. The teacher sees their role as purely academic; their responsibility is to teach knowledge and understanding, nothing more. The teacher is noticeably disinterested in pupils' wider lives and at times is even discourteous, resulting from a desire to ensure that pupils focus on the lesson and its objectives. Although the teacher's transactional view of the teacher–pupil relationship does not acknowledge their wider influence, let us consider what is displayed to pupils in the class: it would be fair to say that this teacher models a lack of respect, civility, and kindness. In addition to the obvious tension with teachers' standards and codes of conduct, the teacher risks teaching pupils that their manner and behaviours are acceptable within the school community.

Many readers will be able to recall teachers they had who embodied aspects of the descriptions provided in Box 2.2.

Box 2.2: How teachers can positively influence pupils through their speech and conduct with pupils, staff, and parents

Speech and communication:

- Ensuring courtesy and politeness of speech (including tone of voice)
- Maintaining positive facial expressions and body language

- Showing support and encouragement/compassionate understanding
- Taking the time to stop and listen
- Showing humility, patience, and kindness
- Being positive.

Conduct:

- Prioritising individuals' welfare, happiness, and wellbeing
- Showing acts of kindness, gratitude, and respect
- Engaging in and encouraging prosocial behaviours
- Maintaining fairness and integrity
- Providing equal opportunities for all
- Demonstrating respect for democracy and respect for authority
- Fostering and celebrating independence, individual differences, and creativity.

Engagement in learning:

- Showing enthusiasm and enjoyment in tasks
- Demonstrating persistence when problem-solving or encountering challenges
- Fostering independence and creativity
- Providing opportunities for all pupils to pursue their interests.

It is interesting to note that both positive and negative experiences with teachers can have an influence on career choices later in life, and that it is often the character of the teacher that is implicated. To illustrate this point, we draw on interviews that two of the authors conducted with pre-service student teachers as part of the Jubilee Centre for Character and Virtues' *Teacher Education* project.[1] When asked to reflect on their own experiences of education, many of the student teachers explained that they were inspired to become teachers because of the positive experiences they had with a teacher (or teachers) during their own schooling; teachers who were approachable, supportive, and cared for them. The student teachers often explained that they had begun their preparation as a teacher, at least in part, because they wanted to emulate certain teachers and support pupils in the way that they had been supported themselves. In contrast, a small number of the student teachers spoke of negative experiences they had with teachers during their own schooling, and highlighted aspects of the teacher's character which caused or contributed to this. Admirably, they explained that they were motivated to teach in order to become positive models for pupils, despite having negative teacher models themselves.

Of course, for many pupils it will be clear when 'good' character is lacking in the models they are provided. They will recognise, based on their other experiences and upbringing, that such behaviours are not desirable or acceptable. However, for younger pupils and those without strong positive models, the modelling of negative behaviours may well have an adverse impact. Albert Bandura's (1977) social learning theory has much relevance to what is being discussed here. Social learning theory proposes that behaviours are learnt through observation and imitation. Learning can be influenced by reinforcements following the behaviour, but it can also occur in the absence of direct reinforcement when learners interact with others (models) within particular environments, including through observation. What we can take from social learning theory is that pupils may emulate the models they are presented with and can learn from how others act and are treated (for example, how another child is praised for kindness or, more negatively, how another child's legitimate view is dismissed out of hand). A teacher who lacks respect, civility, and kindness in their manner, attitudes, and behaviours is unlikely to be one we would want teaching our own children, even if they were effective in enhancing academic progress. On the other hand, we would likely be delighted if our children were taught by a teacher who displays kindness, respect, and compassion. A teacher demonstrating 'good' character virtues such as these not only provides a positive model for pupils but, in doing so, helps to create a positive learning environment in which pupils feel comfortable, safe, respected, and ready to learn.

Teachers' character virtues

So far, the focus of this chapter has been on how the character, conduct, and behaviours of teachers influence pupils. We have been discussing these professional qualities in a reasonably general way – teachers who are kind, honest, compassionate, and so on. It is also important for teachers – and indeed teaching as a profession – to consider more specifically and precisely what the desirable professional qualities of teachers might be. Indeed, it is likely that as you have worked through the chapter, *you* have also been reflecting on what professional qualities *you think* are most relevant to the role of a teacher. In this final main section in the chapter, we draw on the findings of research that presents the character and qualities of 'good' teachers according to teachers at various career stages, as well as three case studies which illustrate character virtues in the teaching profession.

Definitions of a 'good' teacher within the research literature include qualities relating to moral character such as kindness, compassion, and trustworthiness, among others (Tickle, 2001). These characteristics are those associated with the creation of positive learning environments and effective relationships with pupils. To briefly recap some key points raised earlier in this chapter, there is a wide view that 'good' teachers possess more than just the technical skills necessary to transmit information to their pupils (Hansen, 2001; Korthagen, 2004). In addition to subject knowledge, a passion for their subject, and a desire to learn, a 'good' teacher must be of good character – someone who is kind, caring, determined, who has patience and a sense of humour (Arthur et al., 2017b). Pupils tend to share in this perception of a 'good' teacher. In a recent YouGov poll (2018), pupils predominantly described 'good' teachers by discussing themes which relate to moral character: teachers who are kind, who can be trusted, who listen, and who help.

The character virtues and qualities of 'good' teachers form a core part of the recruitment process of schools. When recruiting staff, school leaders will, by and large, actively look for applicants who can demonstrate relevant qualities in addition to applicants who have the necessary skills, or emerging skills, to teach well. It is the character of prospective teachers that often separates successful from unsuccessful candidates. During both informal interviews, for example when visiting a school prior to submitting an application, and formal interviews, an applicant's character is under scrutiny by the school's leadership team. Case Study 2.2 illustrates what prospective teachers can expect during interviews, as well as the virtues and qualities that school leaders actively look for applicants to demonstrate during this process. The character virtues and qualities include:

- Confidence
- Humility
- Teamwork
- Kindness
- Empathy
- Humour
- Good communication.

Case Study 2.2: Recruitment in Schools: The Importance of Character

GARY LEWIS, Chair, Association for Character Education (ACE), UK

As a headteacher of three secondary schools in the East of England for eighteen years, I understood the need for committed staff, both teachers and support staff, who would drive character education. They would do this in their daily interactions with pupils and colleagues and in their determination to ensure that they took every opportunity, both in and outside of the classroom, to consistently reinforce all aspects of our character provision. Apart from a well-resourced and regular commitment to on-going teacher education and personal development, it was obvious to me that we needed a recruitment process which not only allowed access to the best subject teachers available but also enabled us to recruit individuals who shared the school's value system and, by definition, would then promote that value system at every turn.

In addition to my own experience in interviewing thousands of prospective teachers, evidence gleaned from some of the best Schools of Character in England, shows that considerable thought and professional care is invested in organising the interview process to ensure that it is truly effective. Not only will the school have the opportunity to determine the professional competence and values-driven nature of the applicant but the applicant should have ample opportunity to ensure that the community they are seeking to join fulfils all of their expectations around personal development and key values systems. From the nature of a job advert and the content of the prose defining and describing the school community, new teachers should be able to read an advert from a school and immediately understand the ethos and culture of the school.

Typically, a well-constructed interview programme might follow a similar format to that presented below:

- Welcome and introduction to the school involving relaxed meetings with key leaders including the headteacher or principal. During this phase, the content of the day will be carefully explained and the fact that it is very much a two-way process suitably reinforced. Interviewees need to present themselves in a professional manner taking every opportunity to communicate an assertive but empathetic style.
- The school will arrange for a number of opportunities for the candidate to meet with prospective colleagues and pupils. There will almost certainly be a tour of the school led by pupils who will happily provide an honest and frank summary of the school's organisation and culture. These opportunities should be fully exploited and candidates should always remember that they are 'on interview' the moment they enter the school. I used to seek feedback from pupils and colleagues throughout the day assessing the character and likelihood of interviewees to 'fit into the school's way of doing things'.
- During 'non-formal' segments of the day, the candidate should concentrate carefully on how they are communicating with pupils and other staff. Positivity and warm body language is vastly more important than words used and in addition to showing commitment to hard work with a real sense of humour, candidates need to be brave and entirely honest in communicating their personal values, morals, and character traits so that there is no ambiguity. Experience has shown that individuals who remain loyal and truthful to the values which they hold dear are always much more convincing than individuals who adapt their personal presentation in a misguided attempt to 'meet the perceived needs of the school'.
- It is almost impossible to predict the type or nature of questions that might be asked during the interview process. However, candidates should be confident to talk about areas of their life which highlight exactly who they are. Personal experiences and interests described in a manner which reinforces the character traits of the individual, for example, highlighting willingness to lead or work collaboratively with others, affords an opportunity for the interviewer to make an honest and realistic assessment.
- It is not easy to obtain the right balance between humility and self-promotion. However, candidates who are able to provide concrete examples of how they have overcome personal and professional challenges and have shown resilience and determination to succeed, no matter what the obstacle to be overcome, tend to be those teachers who will be able to cope with the multitude of challenges which will inevitably be faced in any classroom.
- Nearly all interviews will involve teaching a sample lesson. I used to enjoy lessons which were pacey, challenging, and threaded with good humour and positive interaction. The sample lesson affords the candidate an opportunity

to interact purposefully with individual pupils, highlighting a willingness to engage in mutually respectful relationships. Ultimately, teaching is all about the quality of relationships that a teacher is able to construct and, as a head-teacher, the ability of a candidate to demonstrate that they were able to adapt their approach and show genuine kindness and empathy with pupils of all aptitudes, was for me a crucial factor in determining their success.

Two reports produced by the Jubilee Centre for Character and Virtues highlight further how good character is perceived in the teaching profession. Arthur et al. (2015b) used the 24 character strengths of the Values in Action (VIA)[2] to help to understand the character strengths attributed to an 'ideal' teacher by teachers at varying stages of their careers. A later study by Arthur et al. (2018) sought to understand how pre-service student teachers perceived the character strengths of a 'good' teacher. While there is not space here to provide a comprehensive overview and comparison of the findings from these two projects, some key findings are provided (if you are interested in learning more about the findings from the projects and how they compare, you are advised to read chapter four of *Ethics and the Good Teacher* (Peterson and Arthur, 2021) and the original sources (see Arthur et al., 2015b, 2018)).

The virtues that teachers perceive as important or relevant in the profession are likely to change with time, experience, and career stage. However, it seems that there is a degree of consensus in the way that an 'ideal' teacher is perceived by teachers at different stages of their careers. Arthur et al. (2015b) asked pre-service student teachers, newly qualified teachers (those in their first year post-qualifying as teachers), and experienced teachers (those with five or more years' teaching experience) to rank the top six character strengths which describe an 'ideal' teacher. Table 2.1 shows the character strengths ranked highest by each group, with fairness, creativity, love of learning, humour, and perseverance featuring in the top six ranked character strengths across groups.

Using a different set of character strengths based on the four types of virtue introduced to you in Chapter 1, Arthur et al. (2018) asked pre-service student teachers to select and rank the top six character strengths which best describe the character of a 'good' teacher at the beginning of their programme (initial survey) and at the end of their programme (post survey). Figure 2.1 shows how pre-service student teachers ranked the top six[3] character strengths at the two time-points. The analysis revealed similarity between the initial survey and post survey for the character strengths of a 'good' teacher. In fact, the same character strengths featured at both time-points (compassion, resilience, reflection, resourcefulness, confidence, and determination) with the exception of *teamwork*, which was included in the post survey. Interestingly, this finding corresponds with the findings of Arthur et al. (2015b): *teamwork* was the only character strength that differed between pre-service student teachers and newly qualified teachers, as can be seen in Table 2.1. This finding suggests that early career teachers recognise and value *teamwork* as an important character

Table 2.1   Top six character strengths of an 'ideal' teacher ranked by pre-service student teachers, newly qualified teachers, and experienced teachers in research by Arthur et al. (2015b)

Pre-service teachers	Newly qualified teachers	Experienced teachers
Fairness	Fairness	Fairness
Creativity	Creativity	Love of learning
Love of learning	Love of learning	Creativity
Humour	Humour	Humour
Leadership	Teamwork	Perseverance
Perseverance	Perseverance	Social intelligence
		Honesty[4]

Figure 2.1   Top six character strengths of a 'good' teacher ranked by pre-service student teachers in research by Arthur et al. (2018)

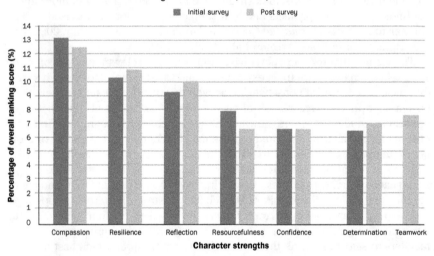

strength. Teamwork is likely to be especially relevant to early career teachers as they take on additional responsibilities and are inducted into their teaching roles.

Reflective Activity 2.4: The character of a 'good' teacher

How would you describe the character of a 'good' teacher? If you had to choose and rank six character strengths or virtues which *best* describe a 'good' teacher, which would you choose and why? Next choose and rank the six which *best* describe your character. Which have you chosen and why? How do these compare to those you attributed to a 'good' teacher?

It is important to note that while ranking measures such as those used in these studies enables us to see which character strengths are prioritised, they do not provide a comprehensive list of character strengths relevant to the profession – if you were asked to rank the top character strengths of a 'good' or 'ideal' teacher you might compose a more extensive list! The final two case studies in this chapter help to highlight some of the other character strengths and qualities that are important to teachers. Case Study 2.3 focuses on in-service student teachers who gain their teaching qualification/accreditation while employed full-time as teachers. As this case study highlights, humility, curiosity, honesty, justice, and respect are all important character virtues needed to successfully navigate teacher preparation. Case Study 2.4 features a personal reflection from a teacher, who considers the importance of character to their own work and life.

Case Study 2.3: Teach First Trainees

Louise Macarthur-Clare, Development Lead, Teach First, UK

As a charity with a focus on ending educational inequality, Teach First places trainees in schools where they can have the biggest impact on disadvantaged pupils. The trainees we recruit have aspirations that align to the Teach First mission and a belief that they have a part to play in supporting that mission. Research has shown that pupils from disadvantaged backgrounds are less likely to succeed in the classroom and go on to higher education than their more advantaged peers, impacting further on social inequality. I have worked at Teach First as a teacher educator for the past five years and have seen hundreds of trainees take their first steps into their teaching career. Whatever their age, background, or motivation to become a teacher, trainees all share in a Teach First experience that helps to shape their character and the character of their pupils.

Unlike most teacher preparation routes, our trainees enter the classroom full-time from the start of the academic year. Trainees receive five weeks of preparation through our summer institute before starting in schools, yet their identities as teachers are only beginning to form at this early stage. Because of this, trainees need to have, and develop, a great deal of confidence. A trainee's new identity grows rapidly as, through reflection, motivation, curiosity, and resourcefulness, they make changes to their practice that ensure that the pupils in their classrooms are making progress. The process of listening to and acting upon the feedback given by a variety of support roles can take humility and determination to move forward. Sometimes, as in all schools in challenging circumstances, pupils come to the classroom and are not fully prepared to learn. This could be because they haven't had breakfast that morning, they have had to get themselves ready for school as their parent works shifts, or they can't see the point in the education that is being provided for them. Dealing with this first requires an understanding and awareness of the community that trainees are serving, and the challenges faced by its families. It also requires compassion from the trainee to understand that the experience of every child they teach is different, and gratitude for the steps forward that are taken, when giant leaps are not always possible.

I have found that as trainees develop their understanding of pupils' needs, they start to realise their influence and position as a role model. Teachers do not just enact character traits in the classroom, they exemplify them at all times. As our trainees make their way towards the later part of their first year of the programme and into the second year as a newly qualified teacher, they start to see the impact they can have on their pupils beyond the attainment of grades. Many realise how they can inspire pupils to have high aspirations for what they can achieve and can become. Sometimes trainees share their own struggles and explain how, through resilience, they progressed despite setbacks. Others overtly teach about and model good character – for example, showing *honesty* to pupils through careful feedback and apologising to pupils if they have got something wrong or mishandled a situation; *justice* when managing behaviour, showing that this is needed even when we think something is unfair; and *respect* to others, showing this even when we are angry or disagree with their point of view. These realisations often mean fundamental changes to the way that the teacher interacts with their pupils, but with this shift comes a more rounded sense of what it means to be a teacher and the impact that they can have on a pupil's life.

Case Study 2.4: Teaching and Character: A Personal Reflection

LAURA HORTON, Classroom and Ward Teacher/Alternative provision in a medical setting, James Brindley Academy, UK

I believe the journey of training and working as a teacher has undoubtedly changed my character for the better. I wanted to join the profession to make a difference to pupils who needed extra support at school for academic, social, emotional, mental, or physical needs. I hoped to cultivate a classroom environment where children could flourish, and perhaps I could too. A teacher's role is more than a job; it is a large part of who I am and has shaped my character and how I interact and navigate my own life.

I currently teach at a hospital as part of an alternative provision. I have the honour of working alongside medical staff to fulfil pupils' personal development and academic needs during a challenging period in their life. My daily work is rewarding and fulfilling as I feel like I am constantly changing and meeting new versions of myself through the pupils I teach. Every day I meet a range of different children with their own needs and personalities along with their families; I often bond with them during their time at the hospital. Something is humbling about being allowed into their world when it is practically falling apart. I get to support pupils and families in ways I never imagined, whether it be as a comedian, a maths teacher, a storyteller, or just for a comforting chat during a difficult day.

Reflecting upon my current practice, the most beneficial skill I am learning is to be present and calm in the teaching moment – to really listen and observe what the pupil is feeling and doing. The next steps come with greater clarity; pupils engage more as it feels like a conversation and the learning moves organically. In the past, I can recall being so nervous, almost frenetic, about getting the timing of the sessions right or thinking about the pupil who just called out, that I was never present in the teaching moment. Undoubtedly, I will have sessions and days like this where I am too 'inside my head' and instructive, but I am certainly noticing the benefits of having the courage to be 'still' in the classroom and let the pupils really actively engage in their learning journey.

A teacher's role cultivates virtues of confidence, empathy, leadership, and communication, but the role equally challenges these virtues. Teaching presents emotional and physical hardship; you work long hours and become emotionally attached to the pupils you teach. The initial character traits I encountered as the most challenging were courage and self-identity. I began my teacher preparation as someone who was quite shy and lacking in confidence; I believed that everyone else had better ideas, a 'larger' personality, and seemingly effortless social skills. However, step by step, I persevered, worked hard, and gained the highest grade I could by applying myself and believing that I could get there too, my way. Over the years, I have realised there are many ways to be a good teacher. I may not be the most extroverted character, but a lecturer once said that I was a 'quiet' teacher, which he believed the teaching profession could benefit from as I brought different qualities to the classroom, as your pupils will. This small conversation stuck, which brings me to the important note on finding 'anchors'. Particularly in my current role, colleagues can provide some of the best examples of generosity, honesty, and working together. I hold these traits to be of the upmost importance as we collectively understand how much working together can benefit each other and can lead to ultimate happiness and fulfilment in the role. By being somebody's 'anchor' and being generous with your time, you not only build firm foundations of friendship, but you also support others simply because it is a good thing to do. For example, I am always there to chat, fix the technology, or recall the name of 'that resource'.

Positive experiences with people can prove just how rewarding teaching is – from when a pupil develops their character because of their experience in the classroom, or when you have completed a challenging term and stand back to reflect upon all the fantastic work a class has produced. Teaching is not a role that you can switch off at the end of the day, as you are always thinking of pupils' wellbeing and progress, and your own personal 'performance' and conduct during the teaching day. Equally, despite the challenges, I adore my job, I am proud of the obstacles I have overcome through sheer determination and perseverance, whilst reflecting proudly on how I have grown as a person.

Conclusion

In this chapter, the focus has been on the character and qualities of teachers. We started by explaining that it is the character of teachers which we often recall when thinking back to our own experiences of education. You have been introduced to how teaching is regarded as a moral endeavour and we explained that in most cases teachers enter the profession as a result of a moral or altruistic motivation. We explored the standards and codes of conduct that teachers must uphold, and you reflected on how the character of the teacher is implicated (explicitly or, more often than not, implicitly) within these standards. We then discussed the influence of teachers as role models for pupils and the impact that teachers can have, even with limited contact time. Finally, we outlined the desirable virtues and qualities of teachers, as well as the character strengths regarded as relevant to 'good' teachers and necessary to succeed in the profession. You were asked to reflect on your own perception of a 'good' teacher and to compare this to how you would describe your character at this stage in your career. This latter task is likely one that you will revisit time and again throughout your career.

Notes

1 https://www.jubileecentre.ac.uk/2937/projects/character-education-research/teacher-education
2 https://www.viacharacter.org/character-strengths
3 Seven character strengths are shown in Fig. 2.1 because two character strengths, *Resourcefulness* and *Confidence*, shared the same overall ranking score in the post survey.
4 Seven character strengths were included because *Social Intelligence* and *Honesty* scored the same.

Further reading

Arthur, J., Fullard, M., Watts, P. and Moller, F. (2018) *Character Perspectives of Student Teachers: Initial Insights*. Birmingham: University of Birmingham, Jubilee Centre for Character and Virtues. [Online.] Available at: https://www.jubileecentre.ac.uk/user-files/jubileecentre/pdf/projects/TransformativeBritain/Character_Perspectives_Student_Teachers.pdf
A research report that presents a number of key findings from a study that sought to understand how student teachers perceive character in teaching, including the virtues of a 'good' teacher.

Peterson, A. and Arthur, J. (2021) *Ethics and the Good Teacher: Character in the Professional Domain*. London: Routledge.
A book that brings together reviews of existing literature and analysis of empirical data from three research projects conducted by the Jubilee Centre for Character and Virtues – The Good Teacher, Schools of Virtue, and Teacher Education – to explore the ethical dimensions of the teaching profession.

Sanderse, W. (2013) The meaning of role modelling in moral and character education, *Journal of Moral Education*, 42 (1): 28–42.
A journal article in which the author examines pedagogical and psychological ideas on what it means for teachers to be role models of and for character.

3 Establishing appropriate learning environments for character education

Introduction

Whether it be as a parent, as a teacher, or as another visitor, our initial impression when we spend time in a school plays an important part in shaping our judgement about what sort of school it is. When we enter the school environment, our senses are immediately heightened; we take in the sights and sounds of the environment as we move across the outdoor spaces, enter buildings, and walk down corridors. Our perceptions of the school environment are increased as we enter and observe what is happening in classrooms. Within moments of entering a classroom, we start to absorb the learning atmosphere, perhaps even imagining what it would be like to be a pupil in the class. How we perceive the ambience of the school will play a large part in whether we believe this environment to be conducive to learning. A school with litter on the grounds, outdated wall displays, and disrespectful behaviour between pupils and staff projects an image of an environment that would constrain both academic learning and personal and social development. A school offering an enthusiastic and polite welcome from office staff, teachers, and pupils, and in which staff and pupils conduct themselves in respectful ways presents a different, and much more positive, sense of the overall learning environment.

How effectively a school is able to shape pupils' academic achievement and personal and social development is in part attributable to a positive learning environment. The learning environment within a school is, in turn, shaped fundamentally by the mission, vision, ethos, and culture of the school. In the introduction to this book, you were introduced to the caught, taught, and sought way of thinking through the formative processes of character education that occur within schools. In this chapter, our focus is on the caught strand of this triad. To recall from the introduction, caught aspects of character are those in and through which 'the school community of both staff and pupils provide the example, culture, and inspirational influence in a positive ethos that motivates and promotes character development' (Jubilee Centre, 2017: 9). The purpose of the chapter is to examine and illustrate how a school's mission, vision, ethos, and culture can create a learning environment conducive to the development of pupils' character. The chapter has three main sections. The first section focuses on mission and vision, including the importance of schools developing *clear* and *shared* statements of intention about the aims and qualities that underpin pupils' personal and social development. The second section builds on the first to consider how mission and vision statements can be translated into the actual ethos and culture of the school. This section identifies a number of elements as being central to bringing statements of intention to life, including positive relationships, meaningful interactions, and modelling – all underpinned by a common language of character. In the third section, some ideas are presented about how individual teachers can further support and sustain ethos and culture within their classrooms and immediate spaces.

Chapter Objectives

By the end of this chapter, you should have:

- Considered the role that caught elements of character education play in establishing an appropriate learning environment
- Understood the importance of establishing clear and shared school mission and vision statements, which include pupils' character development
- Examined how the stated intentions in a school's mission and vision statement can be translated into the lived ethos and culture of the school.

The importance of mission, vision, ethos, and culture

If a school aspires to positively influence pupils' character through character education, it is vital to establish a learning environment that is conducive to character education. Quite rightly, the work of schools involves balancing a range of aims and outcomes – most notably, the academic, employability, and pupils' personal and social development. Throughout this book so far, we have suggested that these various aims are interrelated and that education consists of more than the acquisition of knowledge and the passing of tests. We typically see commitments to each of these aims and outcomes within the mission, vision, ethos, and cultures of schools. School websites, policies, and other documents often contain commitments such as that pupils at the school will 'develop a love of learning', that they will 'learn to be responsible citizens', that they will 'serve their communities', that they will 'develop their academic and vocational abilities', and, as a result, will 'achieve the best they can'. Sometimes, most often within mission and vision statements, these commitments are aspirational. This means that while mission and vision statements are important, they do not necessarily give an authentic sense of what goes on in a school (i.e. the *actual* ethos and culture of the school). For example, the mission and vision statements may sit on a school's website and within promotional material but not actually be used within the school itself. Or, the *intention* of the mission and vision statements may be compromised by detrimental and problematic cultures that actually operate in the school (think, for instance, of a school committed to positive relationships but in which the behaviour of many pupils is out of control). The task is, therefore, not only to produce clear intentions (mission and vision) but also to work to ensure that these intentions are endorsed and enacted throughout all aspects of the school.

Putting character at the heart of a school through mission and vision statements

As Berkowitz (2011a, 2011b, 2021) has argued, a first step in establishing an appropriate learning environment for character education is the development of an authentic school mission and vision, generated by the whole school community. Although in practice such statements fall under a range of banners, including 'aims and values', mission and vision statements provide a school and its wider communities with a clear and concise statement of purpose that helps to identify what is distinctive about the education they provide. An effective mission statement will be clear, and will share the principles and ideals of the school with all stakeholders – including about what kind of human beings the school seeks to develop. Ryan and Bohlin (1999) have stressed that a mission statement must answer the core questions of *who are we* and *what do we stand for*?

The vast majority of schools will have set out their mission and vision. A 2017 Department for Education initiated survey of 880 respondents in England focusing on character education found that 97 per cent of schools had a mission statement setting out the core virtues and/or values and outlining the manner in which the school approached character education (Marshall et al., 2017). This study also evidenced that 'schools reporting highly visible, planned, reflective and specific approaches for character education were more likely to offer a range of provision' (2017: 9). In their study of character education within three schools in England, Arthur et al. (2017a) note that staff identify mission statements as guiding the commitments and actions displayed within the school. In these three schools, the mission and vision statements played a fundamental role in ensuring the clarity, focus, and consistency of the character education provision.

Looking back to Character.org's *11 Principles of Effective Character Education*,[1] we can see just how important a *clear* and *shared* approach is before we even start to think about implementation. Consider just a few of the principles, to which we have added an emphasis on certain key words:

Principle 1: 'core values are *defined*, implemented and embedded in school culture'

Principle 3: 'the school uses a *comprehensive, intentional,* and proactive approach to develop character'

Principle 8: '*all staff share* the responsibility for *developing,* implementing, and modeling character'

Principle 10: 'the *school engages families and community as partners* in the character-building initiative'.

We should also be clear that *involving pupils themselves* in the process forms a core part of developing a clear and shared mission and vision of pupils' character development. A number of studies have found that building school communities committed to the development of character requires pupils to have a stake in the process, for example by sharing ideas about which qualities should be prioritised and how they understand the school as a community (Arthur et al., 2017a; Ryan and Bohlin, 1999). In their 2015 report *Character Nation*, Demos (a leading cross-party think-tank) concluded that a school's mission and vision 'should be developed through a "school community" annual general meeting that includes parents, governors, *pupils,* teachers and non-formal education providers' (Birdwell et al., 2015: 14, emphasis added).

Reflective Activity 3.1: Examining school mission and vision statements

Find the mission and vision statements of five schools, ideally of both primary and secondary schools. These may be schools you know, schools local to you, or a selection of schools returned through an internet search. Locate and extract the mission and vision statements of each of the schools. These statements may not always be labelled 'mission statement' or 'vision statement', but the vast majority (if not all) of schools will have statements that set out the aims and intentions of the education the school provides. Examine the statements you have collected and consider the following questions:

- How do the statements balance various aims of education (including academic learning, preparation for employment, and personal and social development)?
- What values and qualities of character are explicitly mentioned in the statements?
- What similarities and differences are there between the content of the statements, particularly in the values and qualities of character mentioned?
- Do any of the statements give an indication that they were developed by the whole school community?
- Do you find any of the statements more appealing than others? If so, why?
- Put yourself in the position of: (a) a potential parent looking for a school for their child; (b) a teacher applying for teaching posts; and (c) a pupil. What questions would you have for the headteacher/principal of the school based on your reading of their mission and vision statements?

Prioritising a core set of virtues

One question regularly asked by schools and teachers beginning their character education journey is, *what virtues should we choose*? This decision must ultimately be made by a school community. While other schools can undoubtedly provide valuable models for practice, fundamental aspects of character education – including the specific qualities that the school community holds dear – can only truly be determined by the school community itself. It is the various members of a school community – its leaders, its staff, its pupils, its families, its governors, and its community partners – that are best placed to know their context and its needs and, on this basis, can determine a meaningful and contextually relevant list of qualities, or virtues, that speak to and for the community.

As Case Studies 3.1 and 3.2 highlight, no one school is the same as another in either the specific qualities they emphasise, or in the number of qualities they emphasise. Some schools, for example, find it useful to concentrate on a small number of virtues (three or four) to steer pupils' character development, while others will focus on a larger set (sometimes as many as 10 or 12). This is not to say, of course, that schools only focus on their given subset. As we have suggested earlier in this book, schools develop a wider range of qualities, including virtues, that make it difficult to generate comprehensive 'lists'. Focusing on a smaller subset does, however, provide a clear and concise approach for pupils, staff, and families. Think, for example, of a school that alongside a range of other qualities places particular emphasis on the virtues of kindness, honesty, perseverance, and teamwork. Identifying this subset would more easily enable this school to ensure that these virtues are visible throughout all aspects of school life (what a colleague of ours, Tom Harrison, refers to as 'lived not laminated'), including: the physical school environment; school policies (including school development plans); behaviour management strategies; pupil–teacher relationships; assemblies; curriculums; and staff recruitment and retention.

Case Study 3.1: Character Education in the Primary School

SOPHIE MURFIN, CEO, Wise Owl Trust, Manchester, UK

At Wise Owl, our emphasis is on supporting our pupils for life beyond the school gates and this is at the heart and soul of everything we do. Character is both caught and taught within all of our schools. You simply cannot enter one of our sites without both seeing and feeling our Trust values of Resilience, Empathy, Self-awareness, Positivity, Excellence, Communication, and Teamwork, making up the acronym RESPECT.

Throughout all policies, school improvement plans, and documentation, these values feature heavily. Our relationships policy, otherwise known as our behaviour policy, centres around the building of relationships and good character. Good behaviour in our schools is not rewarded unless indicated on an individual tailored plan of support. Otherwise, good behaviour is to be expected in order to build the intrinsic rewards which will be required of our young people when they are making decisions for themselves later in life and in society. We reward our children for displaying good character traits, and these are explicitly pointed out to the children.

The Trust values have also become common language within the schools known by all stakeholders and constantly referred to. We have also developed the language so that everyone knows the meaning of each value and good examples.

Each week our children take part in an activity which has been carefully planned to cater for the needs of the class, with a specific emphasis on one of the values. This is an opportunity for them to explore their character traits in a safe space with adults on hand to coach and mentor. Each activity takes the children on the life journey of an inspirational person, showcasing their strengths and how they overcame challenges.

Children from as young as three take part in these activities. Within the Early Years they are taught through nursery rhymes. For example, the children have a range of puppets that tell stories, introducing and explaining the values to the children. Adults extend these stories by giving the children specific tasks to complete. The children must get Incy Wincy Spider down the drainpipe, overcoming a number of obstacles to test their resilience and positivity. Adults encourage the children to talk about how they could do the task differently next time, and how to self-regulate their own emotions when they get into difficulty. The intended outcome is for the children to understand how to maintain their focus and look for strategies to do this when faced with challenging tasks.

In Key Stage 2, the children walk the Amazon River as inspired by Ed Stafford. They must first work as a team to plan their mission; 'fail to prepare, prepare to fail'. This encourages good problem-solving skills and communication. How will they transport their kit across the river? How can they work as a team to do this? In the dead of night, good communication skills will be essential to maintain the safety of all. In order to ensure that the teaching of character is immersed within the whole curriculum, subjects such as Science and Geography are taught alongside the mission within the classroom. For example, in one mission someone gets bitten by a snake and the team must successfully navigate the doctor to the patient using good teamwork and communication. They must then use ratio and proportion to calculate the amount of antidote to administer. During this exercise, empathy is shown to the patient and all character traits are explicitly pointed out to the children to highlight positive examples.

In upper Key Stage 2, the missions are more challenging and incorporate the character traits required of leaders. In half a term, the Year 6 children trace the steps of Levison Wood, circumnavigating the Arabian Peninsula, travelling over 5,000 miles through thirteen different countries putting to test their character traits. Missions involve the importance of trust when crossing the borders, how to rebuild trust and confidence. One mission looks at the setting up of a charity to support refugees, teaching the children about empathy and compassion.

Other projects explore self-awareness and respect for other religions and beliefs by using the changing of the law in Jeddah to allow women to work and drive as a starting point for discussion and debate.

Time for reflection has been the biggest success within our Trust, allowing children to self-critique themselves, building self-efficacy and self-regulation. It is our belief at Wise Owl Trust that you cannot assess character; however, you can understand your own character traits and growth points, which can lead to a better understanding of oneself and in turn self-acceptance and therefore positive mental health.

Case Study 3.2: Designing Character Education in a Secondary School

LOUISE MACKUIN, Lead in Character Education, Selly Park Girls' School, Birmingham, UK

I am Lead in Character Education at Selly Park Girls' School. I took on the role with the intent of raising the profile of character education in order to develop confident, compassionate pupils who are successful learners, effective contributors to society, and responsible citizens. I wanted to do right by our pupils and so I set out to find the highest quality research and practice. Whilst conducting this search I found the Jubilee Centre for Character and Virtues. I was lucky in that they had just released an online teacher professional development programme which gave me an understanding of what character is, the importance of its development, and guidance on the implementation of character education in a school setting.

Our school has a culture of caring for others and puts the pupil's needs at the heart of everything we do. It was clear from our context that character development for our pupils is crucial to their personal success. Our character approach needed to inform, but also address barriers to pupils' learning and life opportunities; raising their aspirations to take their place in society. We strongly believe our pupils need to be prepared with the skills and attitudes to equip them to make the right decisions in life.

We realised from the outset that we needed to establish a set of universal virtues that the entire community could understand, including staff, parents, and pupils. Our character education programme needed to be relevant to our pupils, and with this in mind the entire school community was involved in the selection of our core virtues. To begin with, we shared a list of virtues and definitions with the whole community. For staff (this included teachers, support staff, senior leadership, and site staff), this was through initial continuing professional development on what 'character' is. We asked staff to select the virtues that they felt were most important. How the selection was made had to be carefully worded: were we asking staff to select virtues which are important to them, or were we selecting virtues which we feel we should all live by as a school community? We facilitated a similar activity with our parents. Parents were given the same question as the staff. We then ran the activity with all of our pupils.

When we analysed the results from across staff, parents, and pupils, it was apparent that there were some virtues that staff, parents, and pupils agreed upon, but others were very different. We decided to form a 'virtue definition' group, to look at the results and make a final decision on ten virtues: Respect, Resilience, Motivation, Courage, Confidence, Aspiration, Reflection, Self-discipline, Service, and Critical Thinking. The group created definitions for each virtue, which were specific to our community, whilst also creating short slogans for each virtue – e.g. Resilience (Accept, Reflect, and Move on; see Fig. 3.1). We also listed three associated virtues for each virtue so that we could expand upon our ten core virtues when necessary.

Following our selection of virtues, we continued to construct and finalise our intent for character education. Next we outlined our vision, and intention for our community via a mission statement. We felt a suitable title was 'Selly Park Promise', as it is exactly that. We also felt we needed a 'tag line' which not only represented our promise but would appeal to staff, parents, and pupils, and would help us launch our new character education initiative. We asked the staff to think of possible tag lines and then voted for the one which we felt would be most applicable for our context. We decided on 'Flourishing Together'.

Once we had decided upon on our core virtues and we had a mission statement, we started to plan for our caught and taught approach to character education. Our aim was to enable pupils to build an understanding of the

Figure 3.1 Selly Park Girls' School's virtue definitions

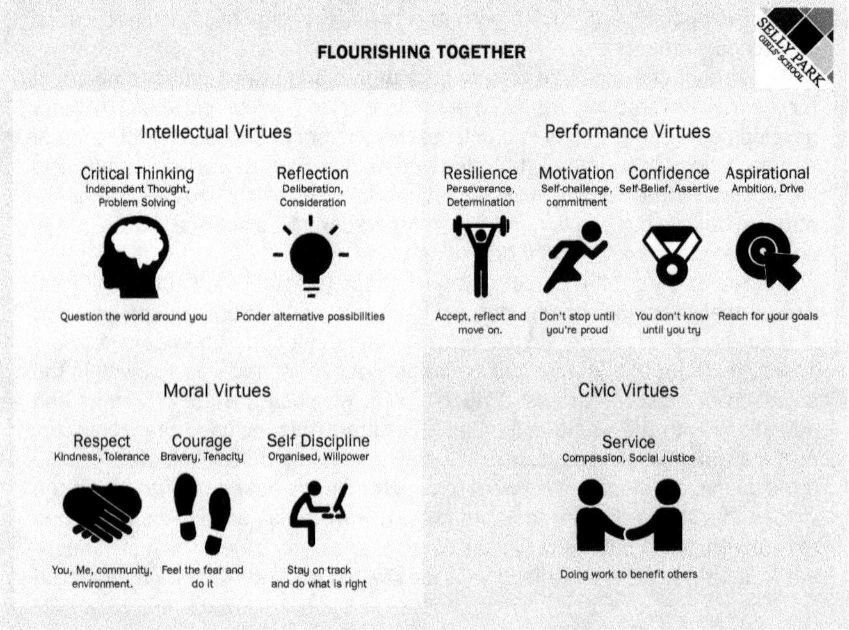

FLOURISHING TOGETHER

Intellectual Virtues

Critical Thinking
Independent Thought, Problem Solving
Question the world around you

Reflection
Deliberation, Consideration
Ponder alternative possibilities

Performance Virtues

Resilience
Perseverance, Determination
Accept, reflect and move on.

Motivation
Self-challenge, commitment
Don't stop until you're proud

Confidence
Self-Belief, Assertive
You don't know until you try

Aspirational
Ambition, Drive
Reach for your goals

Moral Virtues

Respect
Kindness, Tolerance
You, Me, community, environment.

Courage
Bravery, Tenacity
Feel the fear and do it

Self Discipline
Organised, Willpower
Stay on track and do what is right

Civic Virtues

Service
Compassion, Social Justice
Doing work to benefit others

school's core virtues through assemblies, form time activities, reflection tasks, and eventually through all subjects in our curriculum. Our aspiration is for our community to use the language of character every day. We are still early in our character education journey but we have laid solid foundations. We are currently grappling with the question, how do we move from this being a new approach, to being the entire foundation of all we do in school?

Although, as Case Studies 3.1 and 3.2 demonstrate, the school community is best placed to determine the virtues it wishes to emphasise (whether as a subset or as a whole), there are good reasons for ensuring that different types of virtues are included. The Jubilee Centre for Character and Virtues' (2017) *A Framework for Character Education in Schools* recommends that the virtues a school prioritises should include a range of virtues from across the intellectual, moral, civic, and performance building blocks. As we indicated in Chapter 1, in some educational circles – including in some schools – character has come to be equated with the possession of performance virtues, such as grit, resilience, and determination. There has, perhaps, been a tendency for schools to emphasise performance virtues both because they are easier to implement and evaluate, and because many practitioners consider them less controversial than the other virtues (Harrison et al., 2016a). It is inevitable that schools will develop the performance virtues of their pupils, and it is important that they do so. It is also important to remember, however, that performance virtues are not positive and worthwhile in and of themselves. To take an example from current culture and the recent popularity of superhero film genre, the villains in these films often display an abundance of resilience or confidence yet it does not ensure they act virtuously, as these villains lack the moral and civic virtues by which the performance virtues are tethered (Fullard, 2018). Certainly, educators will want their pupils to be resilient and determined, but this resilience and determination needs to be directed in certain ways to be positive – and it is here that the intellectual, moral, and civic virtues are important.

Moving mission and vision into ethos and culture

Once a school has established a clear and shared mission and vision – which includes an explicit focus on pupils' character development – it remains a further task to generate an ethos and culture that enables and supports that mission and vision. Schools are to a large extent made and sustained by their distinctive *ethos* (a word which comes directly from ancient Greek meaning 'character') and culture. In broad terms, the ethos and culture of a school can be understood as referring to the *actual* values, relationships, and conduct that operate consistently in the everyday life of the school. Arriving at precise definitions of 'school ethos' and 'school culture' is not easy, and it is also difficult to pin down what we mean precisely when we say that a school we know of has a 'positive ethos and culture'. When trying to explain this to a friend, we may say things such as 'the staff are all friendly', that 'pupils were on-task and focused on their learning', and that 'staff and pupils were polite and positive in their relations with each other'. Just as often, we may make general statements to describe the ethos and culture, perhaps that 'there was a real buzz in the classrooms', or that 'it is the sort of school I would send my own child to'. The key points here are, first, that in both definition and in practice it can be hard to pinpoint precisely what a positive school ethos and culture consists of, and, second, that what a positive school ethos and culture does consist of is more than the sum of its individual parts. The ethos and culture of a school, in other words, needs to be *experienced* and *felt* to be truly recognised and appreciated.

What we often have in mind when thinking about and describing ethos and culture is the 'climate' or 'atmosphere' of a school. Importantly, school ethos and culture are influenced by, and then in turn influence, much (if not all!) that happens in schools, including: the ability of teachers and pupils to form positive relationships; pupil and staff motivation; pupils' academic achievement and social competence; the extent of teacher collaboration; teachers' attitudes towards their job, including job satisfaction; and the school's reputation and standing with families and local communities. It is, fortunately, very rare for an individual school to have a wholly, or even largely, negative ethos and culture. However, for many schools there will be elements of the ethos and culture which are more positive, and other elements that are less positive, which may detract from positive intentions. For example, high levels of competitiveness within a school community may lead to a 'win at all costs' ethos and culture; and a school in which pupil voice is not welcomed and in which open dialogue in lessons with staff is discouraged, is likely to hinder pupils' understanding of democratic citizenship.

Positive relationships lie at the heart of a constructive ethos and culture within a school. All schools and teachers would argue that they develop positive relationships among staff, pupils, and community partners – but it is the quality, consistency, and direction of these that is most important. Extensive studies into pupil–teacher relationships conducted by Sabol and Pianta (e.g. 2012) have suggested that a positive relationship with at least one responsible adult, not necessarily a parent, is perhaps the single most important element in fostering positive social development, and providing care and a sense of protection, for young people. Positive relationships within schools have been shown to impact upon pupils' socio-emotional development, in-school behaviour, cognitive development, academic achievement, and wellbeing (Hattie, 2009; McLaughlin and Clarke, 2010).

You will recall from Chapter 1 that relationships, within and beyond the school, form a central plank within the PRIMED model for character education. As Berkowitz et al. (2017: 18) have made clear:

> The strategic and intentional nurturing of relationships is foundational for effective practice. School structures and schedules that are dedicated to relationship building must be intentionally implemented to support the formation

of such relationships. All stakeholders and their interrelationships should be included in this relational focus. Schools should connect to and leverage non-school community members and organizations. This includes parent involvement, but also includes local government, local business, law enforcement, community organizations, etc.

The quality of relationships both across and between pupils, staff, and parents will influence the quality of a school ethos. Berkowitz and Hoppe (2009) identified the promotion of inclusivity, where pupils are involved and feel connected to the school, as a significant contributing factor to the development of positive relationships within and across a school. A good deal of research on various forms of, and approaches to, personal and social development emphasise the significance of open communication, peer-learning, dialogical classrooms, and restorative practices for developing and sustaining positive relationships within schools. When looking into the factors that support the development of teacher–pupil relationships, McGrath and Noble (2010: 82) found that schools which have a virtues-led curriculum are more likely to prioritise a school community that has 'compassion, co-operation, acceptance of difference, respect, inclusion, honesty, fairness and responsibility' at their core.

The Jubilee Centre for Character and Virtues' *Schools of Virtue* (Arthur et al., 2017a) study found that pupils placed a high value on positive relationships with teachers, and emphasised that teachers should be friendly and should listen to pupils. The study also found that staff displaying the virtues of kindness and empathy towards pupils through the use of informal conversations was an effective way of building and maintaining positive relationships. Teaching staff across the three schools included within the research also understood that the school's ethos and culture were fundamental in helping them to facilitate the development of positive relationships with pupils. Yet, they also understood that the relationships they formed with pupils were equally important in establishing an appropriate learning environment for character education. In other words, a school's ethos and culture and the development of positive relationships were interrelated and mutually beneficial.

In addition to more formal interactions, it is often the informal interactions that occur within a school that make the most difference to positive relationships. Think for a moment about the interactions a teacher has with a pupil during a school day. Many of these will be formal – instructions for entering a classroom and for completing tasks, taking questions and answers during a lesson, and so on. However, many others will be more informal. These include speaking with pupils before and after lessons, discussing a pupil's involvement in a favourite sport or pastime, when passing pupils around the school premises, and eating lunch with pupils in the dinner hall. The examples and possibilities are many, and it is these more informal interactions that often provide more opportunity for teachers to demonstrate that they are interested in and care about pupils. Now think for a moment about pupils. Once again, many of their interactions with their friends and peers will be formal, such as when they undertake group work in a lesson or participate on a school sports team. Yet, once again, there are a whole range of interactions between pupils within a school that are more informal and which, importantly, say a great deal about the sort of ethos and culture within that school. Once again the list of possibilities is extensive, but we might think immediately about whether pupils are kind in the playground, whether they are courteous in not cutting in line, whether in the changing room they are supportive of the player on their team who missed a vital opportunity to score. Put simply, a school that enables pupils to fulfil their needs for positive relationships will more readily facilitate the acquisition of good character.

Two other core ingredients of effective character education that you were introduced to in Chapter 1 also play a core role in translating a school's mission and vision into a lived ethos and culture – role-modelling and a common language of character. Schools that have developed a successful learning environment for character education have highlighted how staff recognise and embrace their role as both character educators and as role models (Arthur et al., 2017a). Teachers in these schools explain how their school's mission and vision helps them to understand their own role in supporting pupils' character development. As discussed in Chapter 2, the role-modelling of a school's prioritised virtues by staff – and indeed by pupils themselves – contributes to the consistency of a school's approach to character education. In schools with deeply embedded approaches to character education, role-modelling goes hand-in-hand with the use of a common language of character throughout the school and its communities. This shared language provides all members of the school community with the confidence and vocabulary through which they can engage in discussions about

Figure 3.2 Translating mission and vision into ethos and culture – some key elements

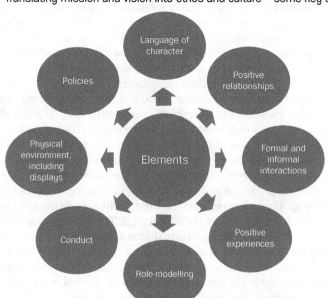

character, including exploring various meanings and understandings of the virtues themselves. Research has suggested that teachers, pupils, and parents view 'virtue language as an essential building block of character, as it provides young people with the tools to articulate their own assessments on their virtue strengths and weaknesses' (Arthur et al., 2014: 19).

When well-developed, the foundations for a common language of character will be established in a school's mission and vision statements and these will then filter through into the everyday life of the school through the various, and not always fully tangible, elements identified here (and set out in Fig. 3.2) that enable the mission and vision of the school to come alive. In the next, and final, section we consider how as an individual teacher you can provide further support of a school's ethos and culture through the physical environment of the classroom.

Supporting and sustaining ethos and culture through the physical environment of the classroom and nearby spaces

So far in this chapter we have concentrated mainly on the mission, vision, ethos, and culture of the whole school. Like others who argue for a character-based approach to pupils' personal and social development, we have suggested that intentional, explicit, and well-defined mission and vision statements form an important and necessary step in creating positive learning environments. We have also emphasised the importance of the mission and vision of a school being a shared project, whether in terms of composition or translation into ethos and culture. In this final section, we set out several ways that individual teachers can support and sustain ethos and culture in the immediate physical environment of their classrooms.

A common theme when establishing an appropriate learning environment for character education is the intentional and deliberate use of a school's physical school environment. A teacher that uses the space at their disposal creatively to display and support key elements of character education will provide pupils – and indeed other staff, parents, and visitors – with opportunities to reinforce and celebrate the school's focus on character. There are, of course, many things to consider when deciding on how best to recognise and celebrate character education within and throughout a school's physical environment. First and foremost, how a teacher makes use of the physical environment must gel with the wider environment within the school. When visiting most schools, we are immediately greeted by a statement of intent; this may be on the outside of the school building but most commonly will be in the school entrance, often coming in the form of a clear display of the school's mission statement, their prioritised virtues, or a combination of the two. This clear visual representation of a school's focus on character sets an immediate tone for individual teachers to replicate in their own physical spaces, such as their classrooms and corridor wall displays. In this way, and similarly to their general conduct, individual teachers play a key role in supporting (or indeed undermining!) the wider ethos and culture of the school. Teachers and other staff in schools are very good at thinking creatively about ways in which the learning environment can be designed and decorated in order to support and celebrate pupil learning – and character education is no exception to this. Described by one secondary school character lead as 'branding', displays in classrooms and corridors remind pupils and visitors of the school's commitment to the character of their pupils. In addition, these displays can also be used as useful teaching tools when discussing character development with pupils, helping, for example, to embed a shared language of character across the school.

The extent to which a school's character education approach is represented in its physical environment depends heavily on the preferences of school staff – particularly the leadership team. Many schools that have developed an intentional and explicit approach to character education have their prioritised virtues displayed. They can be seen in the entrance hall, across the corridors, on glass doors and windows, on bookshelves in the library, climbing up the stairs, within individual classrooms, and across the staff spaces. In these schools, teachers are expected or required to display these virtues – the terms themselves, their definitions, and examples of pupils' work in relation to them – on the walls of their classrooms. Though individual schools may differ in the extent to which they display virtues in the physical environment – and there is no one right approach to the amount of times virtues are displayed – the visualisation can help to ensure that a school's mission and vision statement is consistently represented throughout the school.

Establishing a learning environment through the physical environment of a school is not just about the visual representation of character education through displays and graphics, however. It must also take into account how the physical environment is cared for by staff and pupils. A learning environment which is well-cared for, and about which staff and pupils clearly take pride, can contribute in important ways to the development of an ethos of respect and care. As with other elements of their education and schooling, pupils are more likely to care and take responsibility for the physical environment in the school when they have a clear and direct stake in it – for example, where their work appears on walls, where their successes are celebrated, where they have a voice in décor and equipment, and so on. It is the role of staff within a school to role-model this level of care and respect.

Reflective Activity 3.2: A character education walk

Conduct a 'character education walk' around your school (or a school you are on placement in) and identify any references to character education and/or virtues throughout the school's physical environment. Record the locations of character references across the school and identify the types of virtues mentioned. Refer to the questions below as a guide to help you reflect on your character education walk:

- Does the school display its mission and vision in the physical environment?
- How, and how often, are key virtues/values displayed across the physical environment of the school?
- Are the displays in the school purposeful? If so, how?
- Do individual classrooms and wall displays support the wider mission and vision of the school? If so, how?
- In conducting your walk, did you get a sense that the virtues/values came alive through the interactions, conduct, and relationships you observed?
- If you were describing the school's ethos and culture to a friend, what would you emphasise?

Many of the elements of the character caught approach can be translated into the microcosm of a classroom. As we explored in Chapter 2, one of the most powerful resources you have as a teacher is your own character, and therefore you must be aware of this and use it to help develop meaningful relationships with the pupils in your class. It is generally acknowledged that a 'good' teacher is someone who, alongside having comprehensive subject knowledge and a high level of technical expertise, cares about pupils, and upholds virtues such as honesty, integrity, and justice. Pupils are extremely observant and will very quickly draw conclusions on whether their learning environment is caring and just, and whether their contributions are valued or not. Case Study 3.3 exemplifies how various aspects of school life, including what teachers do in individual classrooms, come together to support and sustain the wider ethos and culture of the school.

Case Study 3.3: A Character-Led Approach at Krishna Avanti Primary School

BINDU RAI, Principal, Krishna Avanti Primary School, Harrow, UK

Within our Hindu faith school, we actively promote values, virtues, and ethics that shape pupils' character, through honouring the teachings of Lord Krishna Chaitanya and those who have gone before us. The faith pervades through the three pillars of educational excellence, character formation, and spiritual insight. Incorporating the National Curriculum in England we provide a broad and balanced model of teaching. Our curriculum includes Sanskrit, yoga, meditation, exploration of western and eastern philosophies and ethics. The golden thread which permeates our teaching is a character-led approach. The Avanti six core universal values – courage, integrity, gratitude, respect, self-discipline, and empathy – are taught and acknowledged by all.

At Krishna Avanti, each classroom displays a 'Tree of Values and Virtues'. Pupils and adults refer to this visual representation when they discuss the learning intention of a unit of work or when they address behaviour for learning styles. It is a constant reminder that for an individual to flourish in society, habits of positive characteristics need to be nurtured, just like the tree needs strong roots and is tolerant to all living things that take shelter in its leaves and branches. Furthermore, the fruit that grows from the tree is shared. Again, pupils develop an appreciation of this when developing skills of stewardship and when understanding that reflection is essential for a growth mindset.

All educators at Krishna Avanti are role models. We consciously demonstrate everyday virtues that encourage our pupils to engage in the deep learning process, emulating and being inspired to adopt the universal values. We expect this from our educators at all times but specifically whilst in their classrooms. Within classrooms, you will hear educators questioning pupils about their behaviours and conduct, by the use of character formation vocabulary. For example, if, during a classroom activity, a child teases another child the educator may say, 'how could you have made a better choice in your behaviour by demonstrating empathy and kindness?' These conversations are deliberate; a reflective dialogue for pupils to consider character attributes intrinsically, helping the pupil to discover the very best of themselves.

Within the classroom we actively encourage our educators to include the skill of reflection, as we feel it is crucial to the process of character development. Therefore, reflection is taught implicitly and explicitly. This leads to an increased awareness and deeper understanding of our values. We have observed that reflection is related to a positive change in pupil behaviour both at school and through parental engagement at home. We aim to develop an atmosphere in our classrooms where educators and pupils avoid the stress of confrontation; creating pupils who feel a sense of responsibility to repair relationships themselves. Our approach complements restorative justice pedagogies.

Educators collaboratively plan lessons that draw upon themes related to character formation. They commence a unit of learning with the 'Big Question' that eventually leads to pupils enquiring about what skills they have learnt and how it is connected to character development. Philosophical questioning allows pupils to develop character values necessary for discernment, right action, and the pursuit of knowledge. This leads to pupils thinking laterally, making connections across subject areas, and developing a repertoire of virtuous terminology. This level of communication is reinforced in the classroom via activities such as collective worship and circle time, as well as displays on walls. Pupils also interact with the Mood Check in Board and their suggestion box. This is where they are encouraged to share their thoughts and character developmental journey through engagement of openness to be reflective learners.

In individual classrooms, peers are encouraged to reward each other when they have demonstrated one of the school's values in their learning at school, at home, or in the community. This has resulted in the transformation of classroom relationships. Finally, through meditation, promoting a vegetarian diet, and yoga, pupils find time to restore, declutter negative thinking, and engage their mind and body, channelling acts of gratitude and personal resourcefulness and goodness.

All these activities inside the classroom empower pupils to flourish and reach their potential both personally and academically.

Conclusion

In this chapter, you have been introduced to the key features of the caught elements of character education. We have traced these elements through three core processes – the mission and vision of the school, the translation and enactment of this mission and vision in the ethos and culture of the school, and the physical environment of classrooms and their nearby spaces. We have suggested that these processes require a collaborative and shared approach involving school leaders, teachers and other staff, pupils, families, and community partners. Whether these processes are in harmony or not will play an important role in dictating whether the aims of the school – including the qualities and virtues the school seeks to educate – permeate throughout the variety of experiences pupils have as members of a school community.

Note

1 https://www.character.org/11-principles-framework

Further reading

Arthur, J., Harrison, T., Burn, E. and Moller, F. (2017) *Schools of Virtue: Character Education in Three Birmingham Schools: Research Report*. Birmingham: University of Birmingham, Jubilee Centre for Character and Virtues. [Online.] Available at: http://www.jubileecentre.ac.uk/userfiles/jubileecentre/pdf/Research%20Reports/Schools-OfVirtueResearchReport.pdf
A research report that examines the intentions, approaches, and methods of three schools taking a pro-active and intentional approach to character education in schools.

Berkowitz, M.W. (2021) *PRIMED for Character Education: Six Design Principles for School Improvement*. New York: Routledge.
Drawing on research evidence and practice in schools, this book brings the core elements of the PRIMED framework to life and gives detailed and insightful accounts of character education.

Harrison, T., Morris, I. and Ryan, J. (2016) *Teaching Character in the Primary Classroom*. London: Sage.
A book that provides a practical guide to why and how character education can be taught in primary schools. Includes a section on character caught.

4 Behaviour for learning: A character-based approach

Introduction

Character and behaviour are intimately connected in the sense that it is character which informs, motivates, and guides our thinking, emotions, and conduct. Developments in the ability of pupils to perceive, understand, and reason about different virtues will ultimately help them to make good decisions, which in turn will lead them to behave in appropriate ways. While schools have varying approaches to character education and behaviour management, it stands to reason that a school focused on developing good character would see this reflected in pupils' behaviour. The aim of this chapter is to illustrate the link between character education and behaviour, and to highlight how teachers can use a character-based approach to build and sustain positive behaviour for learning in schools.

Having read the preceding chapters, you will now be well-versed with the idea that teachers have a vital role in setting, modelling, and reinforcing expectations for pupils' behaviour and conduct in and around the school. Like other elements of character education, good behaviour for learning is seen, felt, and experienced. When viewing schools as prospective parents, as part of job applications, or during other periods spent in schools, visitors can get a real sense of the behaviour of pupils and of how teachers and other staff successfully (or unsuccessfully) manage that behaviour. It is not just in individual classrooms that behaviour management takes place, or that good or poor behaviour is demonstrated. Pupils' behaviour can be observed in, around, and even beyond the school – in corridors, in outdoor spaces, and outside of the school gates.

A whole range of texts and guidebooks exist to help schools and teachers think through and implement behaviour for learning policies and practices. These texts cover underpinning principles and specific strategies that teachers can use in and beyond their classrooms. Broadly speaking, a number of key principles and strategies for behaviour for learning align with character education. Of course, beyond these general principles and strategies, the actual approaches taken to behaviour for learning will often vary from school to school. While schools commonly use rewards and sanctions to encourage good behaviour, they vary in the types of rewards and sanctions used, the balance between rewards and sanctions, the way in which rewards and sanctions are communicated to pupils, and – importantly – the way conflicts are mediated and resolved. Schools which use a character-based approach to behaviour tend to use strategies geared towards developing pupils' intrinsic motivation to behave well and their ability to make good decisions in mediating their own conduct (sometimes referred to as the virtue of self-regulation).

This chapter is divided into four main sections. First, we discuss the relationship between character and good behaviour for learning. Next, we outline the role of school behaviour policies in setting expectations for pupils. We then look at how schools can encourage positive behaviour. The final section addresses some character-based behaviour management approaches. Here (1) character coaching, (2) rewards and sanctions, and (3) reflective and restorative approaches are discussed in relation to how they can address poor behaviour and support the development of positive behaviours. Throughout the chapter, case studies illustrate and exemplify how schools have adopted a character-based approach to behaviour for learning.

Chapter Objectives

By the end of this chapter, you should have:

- Considered the link between character education and good behaviour for learning
- Evaluated how approaches which encourage good behaviour and discourage poor behaviour fit within a character-based approach to behaviour management
- Reflected on your own behaviour management strategies, and how these align with a character-based approach and support behaviour for learning.

Character and good behaviour

The link between character and behaviour is clear when we consider that it is character which informs our thinking, reasoning, and conduct. Bennett (2017: 13) suggests that 'behaviour flows from character, intention and circumstances', acknowledging that situational factors also have a role to play in informing decisions about how to act. When faced with a choice about how to behave or conduct ourselves, good character – and in particular the meta-virtue of practical wisdom – helps us to choose to behave in the right way and for the right reasons. In some cases, this may be a simple choice between following or ignoring a classroom rule. In others, the choice may require careful deliberation and reflection about what to do given the unique circumstances of the situation. To be able to make good decisions, pupils need to be able to recognise and understand the good: they need to be able to notice situations in which virtues are relevant, understand why they are important, and feel motivated to act for the right reasons. It is these aspects which character education seeks to develop in pupils and in this way a character-based approach not only needs to target pupils' understanding and reasoning, but also emotions and intrinsic motivation. Through a character-based approach, pupils are not purely motivated towards good behaviour because of extrinsic rewards or the threat of sanctions; they are more likely to appreciate that a positive action is a good in and of itself, because it is the 'right thing to do'.

We can expect character education to support behaviour for learning, helping pupils to develop virtues across the different building blocks of character. For example, correlations with positive behaviours have been found for character strengths such as perseverance, self-regulation, and prudence in primary and secondary schools (Wagner and Ruch, 2015; Weber and Ruch, 2012). Further examples of character strengths that underpin positive behaviour for learning can be seen in Box 4.1. Interestingly, pupils with tendencies for disruptive behaviour and rule-breaking have been found to be low in character strengths related to self-control: prudence, self-regulation, modesty, honesty, fairness, perseverance, and love of learning (Ruch et al., 2014). It stands to reason that a focus on supporting pupils to develop these character strengths would help to reduce disruptive behaviours and support the development of prosocial behaviours such as helping others and sharing.

Box 4.1: Character strengths underpinning positive behaviour for learning

There are a number of character strengths, or virtues, associated with positive behaviour for learning in schools. These include:

- Respect
- Compassion
- Empathy
- Self-regulation/self-control
- Kindness
- Wisdom/prudence
- Perseverance
- Teamwork
- Civility
- Gratitude
- Honesty
- Responsibility.

More generally, observed behaviour changes resulting from social and emotional programmes and broader character education programmes implemented in schools have been well-documented within the academic literature (see

Diggs and Akos, 2016; Durlak et al., 2011; Jeynes, 2017). In addition to positive associations with academic success, research evidence suggests that character education can have a positive influence on pupils' attitudes and behaviours. Character education programmes are associated with reductions in instances of negative behaviours, such as pupil suspensions, referrals, and lateness; and higher scores in measures of positive attitudes and beliefs relating to pupils' own character, such as a perceived commitment to school and to prosocial behaviours (Diggs and Akos, 2016). Furthermore, character education is associated with increases in self-control, honesty, respect, and social skills; and reductions in bad behaviour, violence, and suspensions (Jeynes, 2017). It is easy to see here how schools might use behavioural indicators as part of their evaluation and assessment of character education – something clearly illustrated in Case Study 4.1.

To help to understand how character education approaches might influence behaviour within schools, teachers might look at aspects of pupils' classroom behaviour, or more generally at school-wide indicators. Ellis and Tod (2018) helpfully outline the learning behaviours that might help teachers to understand improvements in pupils' behaviour for learning, as well as the underpinning attributes that contribute to positive behaviour for learning. The learning behaviours include: how pupils interact with each other and with staff; pupils' attitudes and language used; and what pupils say about themselves, others, and the curriculum. Character strengths that we might attribute to the learning behaviours outlined by Ellis and Tod (2018) include respect, teamwork, civility, self-control, and empathy. For school-wide indicators of changes in behaviour, and indeed the impact of character education, teachers might look at changes to general school statistics such as attendance data, and the number of rewards and sanctions given over time.

Reflective Activity 4.1: Connecting positive behaviour for learning with character

Which three character virtues do you think are most important to support positive behaviour for learning?

- Name the virtues
- Explain why you think these three virtues are more important than others
- Consider what you might plan for in schools to help pupils to develop each virtue.

School behaviour policies

It is the responsibility of teachers and school leaders to expect pupils to behave well (Bennett, 2017). Good behaviour is not only expected because it contributes to good learning, but because it contributes to the development of positive relationships within the school community and beyond. For these reasons, behavioural expectations and approaches to managing behaviour are an important focus of the various bodies responsible for maintaining the quality of teaching and learning in schools. In some countries, it is a government requirement that schools share their approach within a behaviour policy or code of conduct that is usually made available on the school website or via the school office.

Schools use behaviour policies to set out the behavioural expectations of pupils and to communicate the behaviour management strategies used by teachers in the school. Of course, expectations of behaviour are set first and foremost in the home by parents and carers. There is no guarantee that the school's expectations of behaviour will align with those set at home, or that approaches to managing behaviour across these settings will be consistent. However, schools can ensure that they are clear and transparent about their expectations and approaches in the hope that schools and parents can work together effectively. A school behaviour policy may be complemented by a *home–school agreement* in which the expectations of the school, staff, families, and pupils are clearly set out. Each stakeholder may be asked to sign the agreement, acknowledging their role and responsibilities in upholding the school's rules and expectations related to behaviour.

Approaches to behaviour management are increasingly being seen as an important part of the school's wider approach to character education. For example, in schools where there is a character education policy, or a specific character education approach is adopted, it is not unusual to see this reflected within, or as a foundation of, the behaviour policy and approaches to behaviour management. Even in schools where the term *character education* is not explicitly used, it is likely that good character will underpin behaviour management approaches. Schools often base their expectations and approaches on the school values and virtues, which may be set out in their mission statement. Character virtues such as respect, compassion, and self-discipline commonly feature and are likely to be incorporated, explicitly or implicitly, within a school's behaviour policy.

When schools decide to embark on a more focused and explicit approach to character education, they often look to review and revise their behaviour management approaches to align these with their character education provision. Of course, it is unlikely that substantial changes to policy and practice will result in positive changes to behaviour overnight. As illustrated in Case Study 4.1, changes to longstanding practice require time to take root and grow; pupils and staff may need additional support in implementing character-based approaches. What is clear, however, is the potential for character-based approaches to behaviour management to transform behaviour for learning within a school by placing more emphasis on intrinsic motivation, positive relationships, and restorative practices (to which we return below). It is the behavioural outcomes of these approaches, over time, which may indicate the success of character education within a school.

Case Study 4.1: Transforming School Behaviour with a Focus on Character

DAVE WRIGHT, Senior Assistant Headteacher, Aylesford School, Kent, UK

In June 2016, a local authority review deemed the school was failing in every area: behaviour was poor, exclusions were high, and attendance of pupils was below the national average. Teaching staff had started to get frustrated with our school policies – our behaviour policy in particular. For some teachers, the behaviour system worked – they would set a detention and if that did not work, they would email senior management who would take over. This policy only led to the responsibility of managing behaviour being passed on; it also led to poor relationships between staff and pupils. Our real problem was that even with great investment from all staff to make this system work, behaviour in the classroom did not improve. We started to ask ourselves, *does pupil behaviour improve after ten, twenty, or thirty detentions?* – the answer was clearly 'no', yet many of us in teaching seem to think that repeating this type of cycle will inevitably make a difference.

In response to the school's negative review, we started an explicit focus on character education by rebranding our school with a set of ten character strengths. These were chosen by our community stakeholders including staff, pupils, parents, and governors. As a leadership team, we reflected on the ten character strengths and quickly realised it was simply not possible to stick with the current behaviour policy of escalation and punitive sanctions whilst trying to develop these character strengths in pupils and staff. Instead, we needed to focus our energy on building relationships and having high expectations in terms of behaviour for learning. By March 2017, we had scrapped our existing rewards and sanctions policy, stopped using the word 'detention', and replaced it with a character-focused approach to behaviour.

As our entry-level consequence for poor behaviour, we introduced 'repair and rebuild' meetings. These meetings act as a restorative meeting between a teacher and pupil, centred on our character strengths. The meetings help both teachers and pupils to realise how each other are feeling, building relationships whilst also empowering teachers to take ownership of what is happening in their classrooms. These meetings can take place at any time of the day and can be for as long as it takes to move forward. Sometimes the meetings need to take place with other staff in support, or even with parents/carers.

We also use our character strengths as our reward currency and this is communicated clearly to parents/carers at home, reinforcing the idea that demonstrating good character is important at all times. For example, a parent might receive an email saying, 'your child has received a character strength for showing respect today in Mr Wright's maths lessons'.

Throughout this process, we have learnt that the most important thing impacting on pupil behaviour is relationships; how staff interact with pupils and how pupils respond. Some schools, perhaps like ours previously, invest so much time in ensuring consistency of consequences that they forget how complicated the lives and emotions of young people are, intertwined with the constantly changing contexts of home and school. What we have learnt is that consistency in language, values, and teaching is a much more powerful tool in ensuring that we generate pupil commitment and create sustained positive relationships across the school community.

The process of changing our whole-school behaviour policy took time and initially it was difficult for some teachers to move from a purely consequence-based approach, which they had used throughout their careers, to that of a restorative practice approach. It was important that we supported staff during this process, not only on the technical aspects of our new approach to behaviour but also on the character education element of it. During this period, we had to have some difficult conversations with staff about how they should be role-modelling our ten character strengths. As confidence has grown and the impact has been witnessed, we can now say that our staff are fully committed to our behaviour and character education approach, ensuring that this is consistently embedded throughout the school.

In April 2020, we had a school inspection which praised us for our focus on character education, with inspectors commenting on the transformation of the school since its last inspection. In particular, the report stated: 'Leaders have a strong focus on building character education. This has transformed pupils' behaviour and attitudes to learning. Pupils approach their learning positively'. The report also highlighted that leaders at the school 'have high expectations of pupils. They are ambitious for pupils to develop "strong character strengths and reach their academic potential"'. Our commitment to character education runs deeper than meeting inspection requirements, yet such praise has helped to reinforce the importance of what we have been doing to all within the school community.

Like most, if not all schools, we still face challenges in pupils' behaviour – not all of our pupils display good character in and out of school all of the time. However, we can now say that Aylesford is an extremely happy school, where the character strengths desired by the school community are simple, understood, and practised by all. Importantly, when things do not go well – and that still happens – we have a common language and a set of character-driven strengths to fall back on, which support and challenge pupils and staff, and which provide all stakeholders with a framework for our conversations and relationships.

Reflective Activity 4.2: Evaluating expectations for behaviour within your school context

The *Character Education Framework Guidance* (DfE, 2019a) used by schools in England sets out Six Character Benchmarks for good character education provision. The second benchmark explicitly refers to the school's expectations for behaviour and encourages teachers to consider what their expectations are and how these are communicated to pupils.

Use the following questions taken from the guidance to evaluate the expectations for behaviour within a school context with which you are familiar. This might be the school you work at, a school you are on placement at, or one you have been to previously. You might find it helpful to evaluate the school behaviour policy alongside what you have seen in practice.

B. What are our expectations of behaviour towards each other?
- *Are we clear on the importance of discipline and good behaviour in school life? How do we promote this understanding?*
- *How well do we promote consideration and respect towards others (pupils and adults), good manners and courtesy?*
- *How well do we promote a range of positive character traits among pupils?*

(DfE, 2019a: 5)

Encouraging positive behaviour

As we have suggested already, schools and teachers have an important role in encouraging positive behaviour inside and outside of the school. In Chapter 2, we discussed how pupils can learn from what is modelled by teachers and how

Figure 4.1 Contributors to positive behaviour for learning

a teacher's own character and behaviour are essentially important: a teacher who consistently shows good manners, politeness, and respect serves as a positive model for pupils and sets expected standards for pupils. However, teachers can also encourage positive behaviour more directly. For example, positive behaviour can be encouraged through: conversations with pupils – what is discussed with pupils and *how*; the opportunities given to pupils – what pupils get to experience; and through rewards and sanctions – what pupils receive by way of positive or negative responses following certain behaviours. A more expansive list of different approaches which can encourage and support positive behaviour for learning can be seen in Fig. 4.1.

Case Study 4.2: Linking Positive Behaviour to School Mission and Ethos

MEGAN ROBINSON, Headteacher, Elvetham Heath Primary School, Hampshire, UK

At Elvetham Heath Primary School, we believe that teaching pupils the five core virtues of Respect, Responsibility, Perseverance, Honesty, and Kindness is an important part of the curriculum and our positive school ethos. We believe that these five core virtues can be learnt, particularly if we work together with parents to achieve our goals. We believe that everyone in school has the right to be treated as an individual and with respect.

Children's positive behaviour makes a strong contribution to good learning in lessons. Good relationships are vital to the successful working of the school and we expect children to be very supportive of each other in lessons, and to show great consideration of each other's interests around the school. We value achievements of every kind – academic and non-academic – and we believe that everyone should have an equal opportunity to achieve their potential. We also believe that children respond well to high expectations. In our school, we expect everyone to work hard and give their best, to set consistently high standards for themselves so that they need only rare guidance from staff about how to conduct themselves. Our Code of Conduct is no longer a list of school rules; it reflects our character education approach and the language of our five core virtues.

Code of Conduct
At school, children are expected to develop self-discipline, to have regard for other children and adults, and to develop respect for their environment.
Specifically, this means:

- Showing respect – being helpful, respecting property of others, caring for their own belongings, being thoughtful and considerate, letting others enjoy school, and treating adults in a friendly, polite, and respectful way.
- Behaving in a responsible way – responding appropriately to instructions, showing self-control and self-discipline, behaving in a quiet and orderly way within the school, behaving in the playground in a safe, sensible, and controlled manner, being cooperative and attentive in class.

- Observing good manners – being polite and courteous, saying please and thank you. Treating others with kindness and in a way that they would like to be treated.
- Being motivated – understanding and reacting positively to expectations, making the most of their learning opportunities at school and allowing others to do the same.
- Showing perseverance in their learning, sticking at challenges, and developing a growth mindset.
- Being honest in words and actions.

When talking to potential parents who are considering our school, I explain our character education approach and they are very positive about it. Why would you not choose a school that tells you that we work very hard to help children to be the best version of themselves and which focuses on virtues developed by the school community as a basis for guiding and reflecting on pupils' behaviour?

Pupils can learn a great deal about character and behaviour through conversations which focus on character strengths and that use a common language. As you have seen in previous chapters – and as is illustrated in Case Study 4.2 – in schools where character is taught about and understood, pupils and teachers share a common language of character which can be used to discuss and reflect on pupil behaviour. Through character coaching, teachers might refer to the school's specific character strengths when giving praise or explaining the reasons for sanctions, ensuring that pupils understand how their behaviours meet, or fall short of, expectations. In some schools, character passports or journals are used so that pupils and teachers can identify and record: how pupils have demonstrated the character strengths prioritised by the school, the activities that pupils have taken part in, and pupils' personal targets related to character and behaviour. In this way, character passports can be used to facilitate positive conversations about character and behaviour.

Pupils also benefit from opportunities to make good choices and demonstrate positive behaviours through responsibilities entrusted to them. Having an additional responsibility or role within the school can help pupils to develop a sense of leadership and purpose. Importantly, in schools in which character is embedded, pupils are given the opportunity to help others within the school community, aiding in the development of respect, empathy, and service, and helping pupils to see how their own conduct can positively influence others. It is common for schools to set up peer mentoring or 'buddy' systems where older pupils are given a role supporting younger pupils. Other responsibilities and opportunities might include: supporting teachers with classroom jobs (e.g. book or board monitor), taking on school-wide responsibilities or leadership positions (e.g. Eco monitor), being a school council member, prefect, class representative, or contributing to another type of organisation or committee.

Character-based behaviour management approaches

Character coaching

Character coaching is an approach to character education established in the Jubilee Centre's Primary Programme of Study, *Character Education: A Taught Course for 4 to 11 Year Olds* (Smith, 2015). Character coaching focuses on the language a teacher uses, as this has been shown to be an influential tool supporting pupils in understanding the role of virtue in their lives. The Primary Programme of Study explains that:

> Character coaching aims to replace the use of overused and non-specific phrases such as 'well done' or 'good' which do not give any specific indication of what was well done or good. Instead, if a pupil is praised for showing the virtue of determination in completing a piece of work and also given a chance to reflect on their experience of determination, then a link with an enduring character quality is established and any corresponding raising of self-esteem and self-respect will rest on a meaningful platform. (Smith, 2015: 10)

The embedding of character coaching and the inclusion of virtue language in daily interactions with pupils (and between staff) should be viewed as a long-term aspiration of a school. All stakeholders must have a basic knowledge and understanding of the virtues to be able to engage in the process of character coaching. Character coaching cannot be used as a standalone approach to character education but, instead, it can be incorporated into a school's caught and taught approach.

There are three main strategies by which a teacher can initiate character coaching:

1 *Praise*, which involves identifying occasions when a pupil has demonstrated a virtue and helping them to reflect on how that is beneficial to themselves and their community. This form of interaction will help pupils recognise and understand the virtue and to use it again.
2 *Guidance*, which involves supporting pupils to understand the meaning of virtues and to see how they can be applied in different contexts, particularly within a pupil's own life.
3 *Correction*, which involves noticing when a pupil does something that does not contribute towards positive character development. In these situations, correction is not about telling pupils off – it is about helping them understand the impact of their actions and enabling reflection on the virtues they may have used instead.

Rewards and sanctions

The use of rewards and sanctions to promote positive behaviours and pupil engagement is widely advocated within guidance for schools and teachers (see

Bennett, 2017; DfE, 2016; Ellis and Tod, 2018; Steer, 2009). Schools typically incorporate a list of rewards and sanctions, including guidance for their use, within their school behaviour policy. Rewards such as stickers, merits, and other incentives are commonly used to promote and reinforce good behaviour for learning and social interaction. Sanctions such as moving a pupil to a different seat, removing them from the classroom, giving a detention, the loss of break times, and letters/phone calls home, are often used to discourage poor behaviour. Pupils might receive sanctions for breaking school rules or for behaving in ways that do not align with the school's values.

Although it is recommended that schools should use rewards and sanctions to encourage good behaviour and discourage poor behaviour, there are concerns that some rewards and sanctions might undermine character-based approaches to behaviour for learning. For example, extrinsic motivators to behave well can have detrimental effects on long-term behaviour, with research suggesting that rewarding prosocial behaviour can have an adverse effect on subsequent behaviours, especially in very young children (see Warneken and Tomasello, 2008). There is also a concern that the use of external rewards motivates pupils towards the reward as opposed to the achieved behaviour; and that over-reliance on external rewards may undermine character-based approaches, weakening pupils' intrinsic motivation to do the right thing (Character.org, 2018). For this reason, it is important for schools and teachers to direct long-term goals towards the development of behaviours that are not reliant on external rewards (Ellis and Tod, 2018).

However, this is not to say that extrinsic motivators have no place within character-based approaches. The promise of rewards might in fact be useful with pupils, especially younger pupils, who initially require additional encouragement. Pupils may behave in certain ways because of the initial promise of a reward, but through the process may come to realise the importance of the behaviour and the emotional satisfaction associated with this. A pupil who repeatedly volunteers to help because they know they will receive a reward may eventually realise the internal satisfaction of doing good and develop a habit of this behaviour. In this way, rewards can be a useful short-term method for encouraging pupils to engage in positive behaviours.

Reflective Activity 4.3: Moving from extrinsic to intrinsic rewards

When giving rewards for good behaviour in school, how might you encourage subsequent behaviours without the promise of extrinsic rewards?
   You might consider how you would:

- emphasise the character strengths that pupils have shown
- help pupils to recognise the positive outcomes of their behaviour.

It is also important to consider how sanctions might be used to support character-based approaches. Strict consequence-based approaches to managing behaviour typically involve issuing sanctions and increasing the severity of the sanctions imposed with repeated infractions of school rules or standards. While this approach can be effective, it is unlikely that it will address the root causes of poor behaviour (Ellis and Tod, 2018), as shown in Case Study 4.1. Punitive sanctions may alleviate issues in the short term, but without addressing underlying issues and developing positive conduct, poor behaviour is likely to reoccur. For example, a breakdown in a relationship between two pupils, or between a staff member and a pupil, may lead to poor classroom behaviour. While the removal of a pupil from the classroom or the imposition of a detention can serve as a reminder to the pupil about their behaviour, these sanctions, without further deliberation and reflection, are unlikely to be enough to truly address the underlying cause of the poor behaviour.

Rewards and sanctions used within character-based approaches to behaviour for learning are carefully selected so as to support the school's wider character education approach. As outlined at the beginning of this chapter, character-based approaches to behaviour for learning typically seek to develop pupils' internal, intrinsic motivation and influence their ability to make good decisions. Therefore, within a character-based approach rewards and sanctions often aim to:

- develop intrinsic motivation over extrinsic motivation to do the right thing
- provide opportunities for pupils to reflect on behaviour
- provide opportunities for pupils to make amends for poor behaviour.

Character-based rewards

Rewards are often used within a character-based approach to help pupils to realise the intrinsic *and* extrinsic benefits of good behaviour, both to themselves and to others. In schools where behaviour management approaches are based on character, significantly more time is spent acknowledging and praising good behaviour than sanctioning poor behaviour. Pupils might be rewarded when they display the character strengths set out in the school's mission statement or when displaying positive behaviours which reflect these, such as punctuality, high attendance rates, positive attitudes, or increased effort and progress.

It is thought that the use of verbal reinforcement following good behaviours may be particularly conducive to character-based approaches because of the good feeling that is inspired in pupils on receipt of praise. Lickona (2018), for example, suggests that verbal praise and acknowledgement strengthens and reinforces the good feeling that pupils experience from good behaviour, making it more likely that the behaviour will be repeated in the future. When praising good behaviour, teachers can also help pupils to understand how their behaviour benefits others through drawing pupils' attention to the outcomes of good behaviour and discussing how this makes others feel.

Verbal or written rewards are often the predominant type of reward used within a character-based approach. Verbal rewards might include:

- positive verbal praise from school staff
- nominations for school awards
- phone calls home to parents/carers, explaining the pupil's good behaviour.

Written rewards might include:

- star of the week or merits awarded to pupils
- letters or emails sent to parents/carers, explaining the pupil's good behaviour
- commendations from the headteacher or principal.

Verbal and written rewards may also be supplemented with a range of other types of rewards used to promote good behaviour for learning. At some schools, pupils are recognised and rewarded through a points system in which they accumulate character-based reward points, either individually or for their allotted house or team, throughout the year. At the end of the year, pupils' successes may be celebrated in assemblies or specific celebration events. An important part of the process in giving and receiving rewards is that parents/carers are notified about the reward or award and the reasons these have been achieved. Communicating with parents about positive behaviour can be helpful in two ways: first, it makes it more likely that the positive behaviour will be reinforced at home, as well as at school; and second, positive communication with parents may help to develop stronger parent–teacher or home–school partnerships (Harrison et al., 2018).

Character-based sanctions

Sanctions tend to be used less frequently as part of character-based approaches, especially when dealing with low-level disruptive behaviours. Instead of adopting a zero-tolerance approach when classroom behaviours do not meet expectations or align with school rules, teachers might first give pupils time to reflect and an opportunity to make a better choice. In more serious cases, for example when classroom behaviours fall well short of teachers' expectations, when pupils show persistently poor behaviour, or relationships break down, stronger interventions may be necessary in the form of sanctions.

Schools which follow a character-based approach to behaviour are mindful that practical wisdom develops with time and experience. Pupils learn from their successes as well as their mistakes, and for this reason it is important to give pupils time to think about and reflect on their behaviours (we say more about this below), especially when these do not meet the school's expectations. Character-based sanctions used to address moderate instances of poor behaviour tend to emphasise reflection and reparation. Pupils are given the time and space in which to think about their behaviour, to identify what they have done wrong, and, importantly, an opportunity to make amends. In this way, sanctions are not perceived as punitive punishments, but rather as processes which work towards maintaining a positive school environment. Increasingly, schools are adopting *reflective* and *restorative* approaches to deal with behaviour in this way. In the following sub-section, the principles behind reflective and restorative approaches will be addressed and you will be able to see how these types of sanction differ from more traditional sanctions.

Reflective Activity 4.4: Character-based rewards and sanctions

Review how the rewards and sanctions used within a school context you are aware of, or have researched, align with a character-based approach. School-wide rewards and sanctions are often outlined in the school behaviour policy; however, individual teachers may also have their own strategies and it may be helpful to also find out about these by speaking to other members of staff.
    You might like to use the questions below to guide your thinking:

- Do the rewards support the development of good internalised habits?
- Are pupils and their families made aware of how and why the positive behaviour is important?
- Do the sanctions help to get to the root of poor behaviour? And if so, how?
- Do the sanctions give pupils opportunities to reflect on their character and to make amends?

Reflective and restorative approaches

Reflective approaches within wider behaviour for learning practices encourage pupils to think about how their behaviour meets or falls short of the school's expectations, and, more importantly, about the motivations and consequences of their behaviour (both for them and for others). Teachers can support and guide pupil reflection through supportive conversations, and when developmentally ready, pupils might be encouraged to reflect privately. Character passports, or journals, are a useful way of recording behaviour but can also be used to support pupils to reflect on their behaviour. Through directed reflection, pupils are reminded about different character strengths, the school's expectations of them, and their personal conduct and targets. Directed reflection can also give pupils encouragement by reminding them of instances where they were successful in demonstrating positive behaviours.

Restorative approaches are increasingly being used by schools as an alternative to traditional sanctions. Restorative approaches are underpinned by a process known as 'restorative justice', and restorative justice approaches can be used in schools to help address conflict, as well as disruptive and challenging behaviour (see Hopkins, 2002, 2004). Restorative approaches include private conversations that take place outside of lesson times, and schools might refer to these as 'restorative conversations' or 'repair and rebuild' meetings. Restorative approaches are advantageous in that they give pupils and teachers the opportunity to have a respectful and positive conversation about behaviour which can help to strengthen strained relationships. These frank, honest, and respectful conversations help to:

- establish the reasons underpinning behaviour
- uncover thoughts and feelings contributing to the behaviour
- establish who has been affected by the behaviour
- encourage pupils to take responsibility for their actions
- establish how pupils can take positive steps to make amends.

Reflective Activity 4.5: Restorative approaches

Why might restorative approaches be advantageous compared with traditional school sanctions such as removing pupils from lessons, detentions, and other punishments? What are the possible disadvantages? How well do restorative approaches align with core ideas about character education that you have been introduced to throughout this book?

You might consider these questions in relation to:

- pupils' learning
- relationships (teacher–pupil or pupil–pupil)
- long-term effects on behaviour.

Through the restorative conversation process – an example of which is outlined in more detail in Case Study 4.3, teachers and pupils are able to make progress and take positive steps forward. This approach shifts the questions from 'who is to blame?' and 'what is an appropriate punishment?' to 'how can harm can be put right?' and 'what can be learnt so that pupils can make better choices next time?' (Hopkins, 2004). A further and important guiding principle behind restorative approaches is that those who have been affected by the behaviour also have a say in how to find a positive way forward. The approach is conducive to a character-based approach through its consideration of other members of the school community, the focus on honest and respectful conversations, and the opportunity for pupils to reflect on the character strengths they need to work on in order to make better choices in the future.

Case Study 4.3: Behaviour for Learning: A Character-Based Approach

ADRIAN MCLEAN, Character Education and Personal Development Lead, Severn Academies Education Trust, UK

When approaching behaviour management, there is a common perception that a zero-tolerance policy will be the most effective in improving standards. A zero-tolerance policy is one that imposes a punishment for every infraction of a stated rule. In my experience, a zero-tolerance approach does not help to create an environment in which practical wisdom can be fostered.

At Severn Academies Education Trust, we endeavour to use classroom rules based on the principles of good character, with teachers modelling good character for the pupils to observe. Pupils are taught to demonstrate the 'right' type of character by referencing the application of the school values (bespoke to each school) and the expectations of the 3Rs: 'Ready' (to listen and learn), 'Respectful' (of our peers, staff, and environment), and 'Responsible' (for the safety of ourselves and others; and our learning). As pupils progress within our schools, they develop a sense of ownership and self-regulation in how they conduct themselves. However, this is not a quick-fix.

As part of our approach we looked to use restorative conversations. The catalyst for this change was a school community frustrated at seeing the number of detentions rising for issues around poor self-regulation. Data analysis, triangulated with staff and pupil voice, revealed that there was an assumption that pupils knew how to self-regulate. In reality, however, pupils often did not understand why there was an issue, leading to a perception that they had done nothing wrong.

To be effective, whole-school approaches to behaviour management need to have buy-in from all community members, and all staff need to understand the purpose of the approaches. For this reason, we invested a significant amount of time in developing the use of restorative conversations. We sought to ensure that all staff share an understanding about restorative conversations, what they involve, and the character development opportunities that are available through these conversations.

Practice has changed significantly since we started using restorative conversations. Where pupils previously had sanctions imposed on them, they now engage in discussion with adults about why they may want to modify their actions. This has proved instrumental in drawing out the moral and civic character of our pupils. Our restorative conversations firmly place the 'why' at the centre of a semi-structured discussion. The conversations centre around a set of six main questions:

1 What has happened?
2 What were you thinking at the time?
3 Who has been affected?
4 How have they been affected?
5 How did this make people feel?
6 What should we do to put things right or make things better in the future?

Importantly, the conversation process creates a situation where everyone is required to listen empathetically and without interruption or judgement, to both sides of the issue. All parties involved have to be respectful for this to take place. The pupil has to take responsibility for their actions and the impact their behaviour has had. The teacher has to listen to the pupil's viewpoint, encouraging them to express their thoughts and feelings appropriately. Both parties get the opportunity to empathise with their alternate views, thoughts, and feelings on the issue.

We have found that the consistency of the same questions allows the exploration of 'why' an issue has occurred. This facilitates really powerful conversations which centre around character traits and values rather than focusing on the behaviour. A great conversation I witnessed took place around a pupil not completing their classwork. The pupil stated they were stuck and did not know what to do in response to a question. The staff member drew the pupil into a conversation about 'determination' and 'initiative', two of the school's core values. They discussed ways in which the pupil could, in future, display those character traits. The pupil then outlined a solution to the issue, using their initiative and determination to find an answer whilst simultaneously evolving their problem-solving and critical reflection.

A number of pupils previously labelled as 'difficult' have benefited greatly from restorative conversations. The pupils have demonstrated growth in self-esteem and confidence, through feeling heard. This has provided them with an avenue for self-actualisation and positive growth, culminating in them now having a sense of belonging in the school community.

The success of restorative conversations has led us to pilot a similar approach with pupils using 'character conversations'. These revolve around how well pupils perceive themselves to be developing the school's core values and how they can take action to further develop these as well as developing and applying practical wisdom.

Conclusion

In this chapter, we have explored the relationship and link between character education and behaviour for learning. We have looked at how character education, in focusing on the development of character strengths such as kindness, self-control, and respect, can positively contribute to behaviour in schools. We have considered how school behaviour policies explicitly or implicitly refer to the character strengths that pupils are expected to demonstrate, and that their behaviours are evaluated against. We have also outlined how schools and teachers can employ a number of strategies to encourage positive behaviour for learning which do not undermine intrinsic motivation to behave well. Examples of approaches to behaviour management illustrate that rewards and sanctions can be used effectively but must be used carefully and intentionally within a character-based approach.

Further reading

Jeynes, W.H. (2017) A meta-analysis on the relationship between character education and student achievement and behavioral outcomes, *Education and Urban Society*, 49 (1): 1–39.
A journal article presenting the results of an extensive meta-analysis of 52 studies focusing on the relationship between character education, student achievement and out-

comes. The findings suggest that character education is associated with higher levels of love, integrity, compassion, and self-discipline.

Weber, M. and Ruch, W. (2012) The role of a good character in 12-year-old school children: Do character strengths matter in the classroom?, *Child Indicators Research*, 5 (2): 317–334.

A journal article that presents the results of a study looking at the associations between good character at school and a range of outcomes, including positive classroom behaviour. The study used the Values in Action Inventory of Strengths as well as teacher ratings.

5 | Teaching character education within and across the curriculum

Introduction

As explained in the introduction to this book, in many countries character education (and indeed personal and social development more widely) does not have a formal curriculum, enabling schools and teachers to channel their skills, passions, and motivations to design and plan character education in a way tailored to their school. Even where curriculum standards are in place, schools and teachers have a degree of freedom and flexibility in how they implement these standards. As you will see throughout this chapter, schools that have developed intentional and clearly planned forms of character education typically demonstrate a freedom to be creative and responsive within and to their school community, and this includes how they handle the taught elements of character.

When school leaders and teachers design their character education provision, it is important they remember that there is no 'one-size-fits-all' formula that will work across all schools or educational settings. While there are similarities between schools, each school has its own distinctive characteristics and needs, and these contexts should inform the precise methods and teaching and learning approaches taken. The aim of this chapter is to provide examples of teaching and learning approaches to character education in order to illustrate how subtle changes to planning and practice can enable a more explicit and developed focus on character education. The teaching and learning approaches covered are by no means an exhaustive list (in the concluding chapter of this book, we provide a list of further resources that you can investigate), but they will provide valuable insight into how schools can – and indeed have – successfully approached character development.

Our intentions in the chapter, exemplified through the various case studies included, are twofold: first, to emphasise good practice and, second, to highlight that many of these teaching and learning approaches align with existing methods and practices used commonly within schools. For example, it would be difficult to find:

- a primary school teacher who has not discussed the character of protagonists – or about character strengths such as honesty – when using a story as a teaching tool or when teaching a particular text as part of a lesson;

- a physical education teacher who has not mentioned the importance of teamwork and determination;
- a history or geography teacher who has not developed curiosity, empathy and reflection in their pupils; or
- a creative arts teacher who has not sought to inspire creativity.

The chapter consists of three main sections. The first sets out what we mean by both character taught and the curriculum. In the second section, we examine ways that character can be taught through curriculum subjects. While not an exhaustive list, we set out links that can be made to character within a number of subjects and subject areas. In the third main section, we broaden out the 'curriculum' to consider how character education connects to the wider curriculum in schools. Here, we focus on form/home groups, assemblies, and enrichment before, in the next chapter, moving on to consider social action. One final note by way of introduction is needed. While we make some comments about differences between primary and secondary schools here, the teaching and learning approaches presented are relevant to younger and older children alike. This does not mean that teaching and learning approaches do not need to be moulded to the ages and abilities of the pupils being taught, but rather that the approaches, methods, and strategies examined here can be designed and implemented in ways tailored to the needs of all pupils. Teachers and schools will invariably adapt their teaching and learning approaches to meet pupils' needs, and character education is no different to other aspects of education in needing to track and be informed by the precise needs of pupils.

Chapter Objectives

By the end of this chapter, you should have:

- Considered the importance of incorporating character education within and across a school's curriculum
- Understood different approaches by which character education can be taught within and across the curriculum
- Reflected on real-life examples of a character taught approach and considered how you will approach teaching character in your setting.

Character taught and the 'curriculum'

A taught approach to character education does not sit in isolation from caught and sought methods of character education, which develop character most notably through a school's vision, ethos, and culture. The view that character can be taught as an explicit element of character education recognises that the 'direct teaching of character provides the rationale, language and tools to use in developing character elsewhere in and out of school' (Jubilee Centre, 2017: 3). In other words, if pupils are to make sense of, learn about, and act in accordance with the mission of the school, the school needs to provide:

> educational experiences in and out of the classroom that equip students with the language, knowledge, understanding, skills and attributes that enable character development. (Jubilee Centre, 2017: 9)

The curriculum stands as a key tool to both focus and enable the taught elements of character education, but what is a curriculum? On the surface this seems a fairly simple question, but it is much more complex. This is because all schools and teachers will be working with a number of curriculums. On a narrow view, a curriculum is a formal categorisation of the knowledge, skills, and dispositions that pupils are to be taught and are to learn. We might talk, for example, about the official, statutory curriculum for a particular subject. At the level of the school, the curriculum may refer to the units of work, lesson plans, and other materials and resources that structure teaching and learning. On a wider view, the curriculum refers to all learning experiences within the school, including formal and informal learning. When discussing the purpose of education, Biesta (2015: 80) has argued that a school's curriculum should be 'flexible, personalised, and tailored to individual students' but at times also 'strict, structured, and general'. Biesta, again, highlights the complexity of curriculum design by arguing that in some examples a school curriculum 'needs to be centred on the student – for example, when we want to promote creative action and generative thinking – but sometimes it needs to be centred on the teacher'. We can also think of the curriculum as the overarching framework of children's education and as a statement of what knowledge, skills, and moral principles pupils ought to acquire during their time at school (Ryan and Bohlin, 1999).

The most common way that schools and teachers *work with* curriculums is through their planned courses of study. It is through these planned courses, which operate at year and subject levels, that teachers interpret and implement relevant national/local education standards, including any statutory requirements that are in place. Beyond these more formalised curriculums stand those extra-curricular activities, including sports, drama, social action, and other enrichment activities that enable schools to provide a holistic and well-rounded curriculum. Through planning and implementing these curriculums, teachers can also incorporate and emphasise the knowledge, understanding, and dispositions that they and the wider school community wish to include.

As a whole, the formal curriculum is one of the tools by which a school's ethos and culture is physically manifested, and the curriculums within a school make a statement about the type of character development a school wishes to see within their pupils. Teachers invest large amounts of time and effort in a commitment to design curriculums that serve all of their pupils. With schools feeling under continued pressure to analyse and measure all elements of their curriculums, it is easy for schools to focus largely on their formal curriculum and to concentrate more narrowly on the academic knowledge and skills they wish pupils to learn.

So where does character education fit into the formal curriculum? In one sense, character education can be everywhere. However, there is no magic blueprint, meaning that schools and teachers have to think very carefully about how character is developed within and across the curriculum. It is very rare for character education to feature as a discrete and specific subject, meaning that when character is taught 'within and across the curriculum', this largely refers to the explicit teaching of virtues and character strengths through existing curriculum subjects, through form/home/pastoral sessions, and through assemblies. When this occurs, and as the case studies throughout this chapter highlight, as with any aspect of curriculums, it is essential that the development of character education is made intentional and explicit through careful planning and design. Case Study 5.1 provides a snapshot of how one school has developed their approach to the taught elements of character education.

Case Study 5.1: Personal Development and Welfare Lessons at Ark Boulton Academy

HARLEEN KAUR ASSI, Assistant Principal (Character Development & Pastoral Care), Ark Boulton Academy, Birmingham, UK

In 2014, a school inspection deemed a long-standing inner-city school in Birmingham, England, to be inadequate. Urgent remedial action was required for sustained change, and character education became the much-needed anchor for the parents, pupils, teachers, and stakeholders of the newly branded Ark Boulton Academy. The mission statement of 'It takes a whole community to raise a child' laid the foundations for an ethos and culture with character education at the heart of every interaction.

To put our mission into practice at Ark Boulton, weekly curriculum time is dedicated to all year groups to enable pupils to develop a deep understanding of virtuous concepts in the form of Personal Development and Welfare lessons. These lessons are taught using the same pedagogy as other lessons, and are planned and delivered with the same rigour of teaching and learning as all other subjects. Teachers intellectually prepare for the lessons by participating in professional development through a Professional Learning Community model which supports staff in exploring complex issues. Training in delivering Personal Development lessons is given a dedicated slot each week and Personal Tutors build knowledge, confidence, and delivery of subject content by scripting model answers and identifying potential misconceptions.

To put this thinking into context for our pupils, a key pedagogical approach to Personal Development lessons at Ark Boulton is to 'narrate the thinking' of the source or stimulus. Here, teachers methodically extrapolate key information from stimulus material to draw out the virtuous behaviour that we aspire to. Subsequently, pupils are able to consider this detail in a 'Think Pair Share' activity, where they put their oracy skills to the test in speaking and presenting to their peers.

Lessons in the Personal Development and Welfare curriculum are informed by moral virtues and research in character education from academic journals, articles, books, and research studies. This is important because morals and virtuous dispositions go beyond single communities or isolated issues in society. They are not based on people's perceptions or philosophies of how to live their lives in the easiest way or where they have the most to gain from others. At Ark Boulton, it is our belief that virtuous thinking, belief, and actions transcend individuals and communities and therefore society collectively flourishes.

Our character education content is sequenced to focus upon topics that affect young people today. These include respectful conversations, being a good online citizen, valuing education, compassionate listening, emotional wellbeing, the importance of sleep, and how to prevent conflict, resolve conflict, and forgive after conflict. Topics specific to our community include knife crime, gangs and violence, extortion and money fraud to name a few.

Furthermore, statutory requirements in PSHE, SMSC, SRE, as well as localised issues that reflect the make-up of the school community are all integrated into Personal Development lessons. Taking litter in the local community as an example, we facilitate discussion and debate, using the language of virtues such as 'compassion' for the environment. We then teach our pupils about the laws around littering, how council-led refuse and recycling collections work, and how to report fly tipping. This is followed with the Ark Boulton Community Clean event where pupils wear high-visibility jackets alongside teachers and clean streets in the local community. We carry out an environmental survey of the local park and contact MPs to improve features in the area.

It is impossible to assess pupils' authentic progress in virtuous behaviour, so we do the next best thing; pupils deliver an exposition to their class about the virtues they have researched, been taught, and practised. We provide a grade on content and delivery of their speech. Teachers standardise and improve practice by carrying out moderation in marking and feedback of pupil expositions just as they would in any other curriculum area.

Over time, character education has enabled the enactment of the school mission, 'It takes a whole community to raise a child', to become part of our school culture and ethos. Learning how to be virtuous does not just come from a theoretical classroom-based series of tasks. It is coupled with planned and intentional opportunities in school to practise the application of virtues on a daily basis, guided by teacher role models. This provides a tool kit by which every child is empowered with, and will stay with them beyond the school gates.

Careful planning and design allows for consistency across language, style, content, and topics, ensuring the teachers and pupils can not only make sense of the emphases on character, but can make connections between these – including to the wider character caught emphasis within the school. It is important when designing and planning character education within and across the curriculum that the lessons and topics by which the virtues are taught are age-appropriate. Clearly, in a primary school it would be unrealistic to expect a Year 1 pupil to have the same level of knowledge and understanding as a Year 6 pupil, just as in a secondary school there would be different expectations of a Year 10 pupil to that of a Year 7 pupil. This is not to say that conversations about character and virtues cannot occur with younger pupils, but it is to suggest that a considered progression of the language of character and the depth of attention to the key components of virtue must be planned sensitively.

A character education curriculum should be interesting and meaningful to pupils, and should provide opportunities for pupils to reflect on what they are learning in the context of their own lives. While there is no exact pathway to follow – teachers in schools will know their contexts and their pupils' individual needs best – a consistently recommended approach to curriculum design and planning for character education is the *spiral curriculum* (Arthur et al., 2017c; Wright et al., 2014).

The spiral curriculum approach to character education is inspired by Jerome Bruner's Spiral Curriculum (Bruner, 1960). In their *Character Education: A Taught Course for 11 to 16 Year Olds*, Wright et al. (2014: 7) explain that:

> the spiral curriculum model moves pupils through phases of personal experience and practice, information gathering and documentation, reflection, analysis and internalisation and informed action, and round again, as if moving up a spiral. This enables pupils to look at previous learning and experience in a new light, and look at new learning from the perspective of previous experience. Growth in knowledge, judgement and practice is the purpose of such an approach.

As can be seen from Fig. 5.1, the spiral curriculum model enables pupil growth through an ongoing cycle of: 'personal experience and practice', 'information gathering and documentation', 'reflection and analysis, and formulation of personal theories', and 'informed action'.

As illustrated in Fig. 5.2 and Reflective Activity 5.1, the spiral curriculum model can also translate into and inspire the design of sequences of teaching and learning, including individual lesson plans.

Teaching character through subjects

Developing character within and through existing subject-based curriculums enables pupils to develop a deeper understanding of character and its relevance. Existing subjects, whether in primary or secondary schools, provide a ground of familiarity for pupils from which they can make connections to character, allowing teachers to facilitate pupils' knowledge and reflection (Harrison et al., 2016b).

When examined closely, there are many implicit links to the teaching of virtues which run throughout the primary and secondary subject curriculums; therefore, and as Case Study 5.2 illustrates, only minor adjustments need to be made to make these links more explicit within the content of individual lessons and wider units of learning. However, it is not just within the curriculum

Figure 5.1 A spiral curriculum model (Wright et al., 2014: 7)

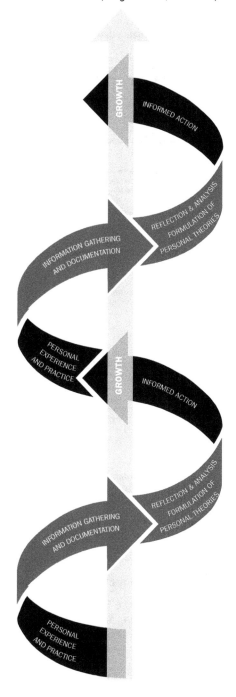

Figure 5.2 Planning a character-focused lesson – a stepped approach

Step 1: Identify the virtue(s) of focus and how these connect to other knowledge and skills being developed in the lesson

It is recommended that, within the initial stages of a character education approach, lessons focus on no more than one or two virtues. As pupils' knowledge and understanding of character virtues develops, this may increase and clusters of virtues may be taught in tandem.

Step 2: Identify a component of virtue

Select a component(s) of virtue (see Chapter 1) on which to base a learning objective. This will provide a clear focus for a character education lesson and will support teachers when evaluating the impact of the lesson.

Step 3: Consider prior knowledge and personal experience

Ensure you are aware of pupils' previous learning related to the virtue(s) you are teaching. For example, are pupils able to define the meaning of the virtue(s)? Can pupils notice situations involving or in need of the virtue(s)?

Step 4: Plan activities, including the experiential

Teacher- and pupil-led activities should help pupils to achieve the learning objective and work towards the corresponding component(s) of virtue. Teachers can use different approaches to facilitate discussion about the virtue(s) in focus. Teachers may need to differentiate to best suit their pupils' needs; paired, shared, group or guided work are encouraged.

Step 5: Give room for reflection

It is important that pupils are given opportunities to reflect. Reflection activities should help pupils to relate the virtue to their own lives and experiences.

Reflective Activity 5.1: Planning a character-focused lesson

Using the stepped approach from Figure 5.2, plan a character-focused lesson that concentrates on a specific virtue, e.g. courage or generosity. Consider planning activities that focus on developing pupils' virtue perception, virtue knowledge and understanding, and virtue reasoning.

content that pupils' character development occurs; the pedagogical practices teachers employ within individual subjects also play an important role. As Arthur et al. (2017c: 81) have suggested, 'teachers should encourage pupils to discuss and debate issues of morality, ethics and character that come up in their subjects in a critically reflective way'. Included within this pedagogical approach, where possible, teachers should try to provide real-life examples, linked to their subject content, which in turn will encourage pupils to discuss and reflect on their character development in relation to issues, events, and questions which are more relevant to their own lives – as again illustrated in Case Study 5.2.

Case Study 5.2: Teaching Character through Subjects

MATTHEW BAWDEN, Assistant Headteacher, Queen Elizabeth's Grammar School, Ashbourne, UK

The best schools offer guided opportunities to catch character, to seek out ways to develop character, and lessons and activities where character development can be taught. By working on a resource for teachers called *Teaching Character Through Subjects*, I was able to source some fantastic practice from across England. Much of this is now embedded in my own setting. We began by mapping the opportunities that were already there and making these more explicit. Since then we have actively looked for new opportunities and built the curricular links to make them work. Even then, these links are not worth a lot without genuine pupil buy-in. Involving pupil leadership from the beginning ensures everyone makes the most of their in-lesson learning experiences.

An excellent character resource found in one subject is often easily transferable to another. From experience, opportunities and resources tend to fall into one of a couple of categories. Some lessons use character development as a mechanism for increasing subject learning, and in so doing develop character. These present opportunities for pupils and staff to see how activities, such as conducting independent learning around circle theorems, can help pupils develop an understanding of specific character virtues. Other lessons might focus more on the character virtues, but in a subject context. Here the emphasis is on how the lesson can support the development of one or more virtues. A short series of lessons in PE, for example, where the explicit objective is to refine virtues linking to team-building, can provide the pupils and staff with an invaluable context for their character education.

Schools often focus on independent learning and team-building. Scaffolding such things around character virtues, or changing the focus to tackle virtues 'head-on', adds a significant depth to the activities. This enables the learning to resonate with all of those who participate. Any subject teacher and department expressing a wider interest in pupils will always have more success. Likewise, any pupil who feels the subject teacher and department cares and wants to help them develop will behave better, try harder, and wish to be in the room, lab, or on the pitch. Mental health and wellbeing also appears to improve when pupils feel their personal development is valued in all areas of school life.

To this end, it is important to step beyond the subjects and look for the cross-curricular links. A character development technique that works in Maths, and appears again in French, leads to pupils seeing their development across more subjects, and not viewing them in isolation: 'oh, we do character in Maths' becomes 'we learn about character in school'. Similarly, a subject that uses character education to reach out beyond the gates can harness even greater opportunities. Maths and Languages in my setting both reach out to Westminster School in Sharjah, offering lessons focused around such things as character, chess, and Arabic. By sharing character development experiences, it is hoped pupils will see their desire to develop in both our local environment and more globally.

While at first glance the task of incorporating a character focus in subject teaching may seem daunting (or indeed 'yet another thing to do'), on closer inspection all curriculum subjects offer a variety of possibilities. Given this, it is not possible in the space available to set out all of the possible ways that character can be given explicit attention within subjects and subject areas. In the concluding chapter to this book, we provide a list of further resources, some of which include practical guides and programmes for teaching character in and through curriculum subjects. In the remainder of this section, we present in table form (Table 5.1) and through two case studies (Case Study 5.3 and Case Study 5.4), some ideas and practical applications of teaching character through subjects.

Case Study 5.3: Character Education through English

LILIKA BEGUM, English Teacher, Northampton Academy, Northampton, UK

Northampton Academy is a school of character where respect, determination, ambition, integrity, and tolerance are our foundation. In recent years, we have been integrating character education into our curriculum to cultivate character values in our pupils, and as an English teacher this has added meaningful reflection to our lessons and given way to greater personal growth alongside academic success. You will find there are countless ways to facilitate character development in English, and some examples of how we teach character are detailed below.

Our Year 7 pupils have the opportunity to engage with character education in English during their first term, using our scheme: 'Around the World in Seven Values'– the first five of which are core to our school. The scheme of work comprises seven fictional extracts, taken from authors with diverse backgrounds and viewpoints who best represent the world our pupils live in. Week by week, pupils use an extract to investigate how a character value is defined, applied, challenged, and sometimes conflicted. We break ground with the moral virtue of respect, understand its meaning, share our own experiences and contemplate its importance. Importantly, we then study how respect is lacking in a conversation taken from Blackman's *Noughts and Crosses*. We ask and answer: what words or phrases show respect? Which don't? What could these words convey instead? How does this reflect on Sephy and Callum's characterisation? Why would Blackman explore respect in this way? Of course this develops vital reading and analytical skills, however as the focus incorporates character pupils develop virtue literacy and allow themselves to consider bigger questions, for example how the presence of respect can control a conversation or how respect can be restricted by status.

In later lessons, we evaluate perspectives with character at heart. When gathering our ideas, for example, pupils assess the values needed to create a community, how values expressed by certain figures threaten this, and what the purpose of this contrast could be. While uncovering layers of meaning and the author's intent, pupils begin to link values in a network and with each cumulative week, begin to perceive values as complex, malleable, and dependent on each other.

We also develop pupils' writing skills through a focus on character and characterisation of protagonists in stories. After pupils have designed their literary character's defining features, we ask them to place this character in a character-testing situation. For example, the character might find an engagement ring on the pavement and notice a person searching among the fallen leaves. We would ask pupils to discuss, justify, and debate how their character would act in this situation – in this case, focusing on the *integrity* of the character – so as to introduce the idea of an author's intent. Once we have discussed the different options available in the scenario (which may or may not evidence the benefits of showing integrity), we focus on describing every detailed moment that reveals something about the character's integrity. This technique can be used with different year groups, but does rely on core writing skills being in place, before embedding this level of detailed character education.

Through activities like this, pupils can explore the idea of an author's intent and learn to craft insightful characterisations. The exercise gives pupils the ability to manipulate the connection between a person's value system and their actions, while reflecting on their own character. I have found this brings about more thoughtful consideration when discussing the behaviour of literary characters as well as those the pupils create in their descriptive pieces of writing.

Table 5.1 Links to character in subject areas/subjects

Subject area/ subjects	Key connections	Example virtues in focus	Elaboration
Computer Science	Computer Science should not only concentrate on technical knowledge and skills, but also on key ethical issues, such as those associated with the emergence of new technologies One of the core aims of the Computer Science curriculum should be to contribute towards the development of digitally wise young people who are able to safely and ethically navigate the ever-expanding cyberspace	communication confidence courage creativity critical thinking determination honesty justice kindness resilience	Discussions on how to use technology safely and respectfully, including keeping personal information private and identifying where to go for help and support on the internet, can provide opportunities to discuss honesty, courage, and appropriate, kind communication Applying the fundamental principles and concepts of Computer Science, including abstraction, logic, algorithms, and data representation demonstrates critical thinking and creativity
Creative Arts (Art, Drama, Music, and Photography)	Creative Arts should engage, inspire, and challenge pupils to invent and create their own works of art. Pupils' creative art should not only reflect the great artists they try to emulate but also express and develop who pupils are as individuals	ambition courage creativity curiosity determination empathy humility perseverance reflection respect	To develop a true understanding of the historical and cultural significance of great artists and designers, pupils should be encouraged to reflect on these art forms with respect and empathy Pupils must be made aware that to become proficient in numerous artistic techniques, such as drawing, painting, and sculpture, takes determination and perseverance over an extended period of time Drama offers opportunities for pupils to understand and explore characters, including through role-play, helping to develop empathy and respect

Subject area/ subjects	Key connections	Example virtues in focus	Elaboration
			In music, pupils compose, create, and perform in solo and ensemble contexts, developing and expressing the virtues of confidence, determination, communication, and teamwork. Pupils can be provided opportunities for discussions and reflections on character, for example through the lyrics of chosen songs
Design and Technology	Design and Technology is more than just a subject that teaches pupils the technical and practical skills needed to create useful products. For a design or product to be successful, a pupil must also study and understand what people really like, what they think, and how they behave. Pupils should also learn about the ethical dimensions of product design and manufacture	confidence creativity curiosity empathy honesty resilience resourcefulness respect teamwork	Producing solutions to practical design problems with limited resources or under constraints can be a valuable way to teach resourcefulness and encourage creativity Whilst evaluating and testing their ideas and products, along with the work of others, pupils will need to demonstrate honesty and a respect for the opinions of others
Humanities and Social Sciences (including History, Geography, and Citizenship/ Social Studies)	One of the core aims of History is to explore and understand different periods, times, and cultures, providing countless opportunities to focus explicitly on themes relevant to character development. Through the use of historical sources, pupils can engage with alternative views and teachers can use these sources to construct debates around ethical dilemmas of the past and present	civility compassion empathy justice leadership resilience respect service teamwork volunteering	The exploration of significant individuals in the past who have contributed to national and international achievements enables pupils to consider the moral dilemmas and decision-making of said figures as well as identifying their core character virtues

(continued)

Table 5.1 (continued)

Subject area/ subjects	Key connections	Example virtues in focus	Elaboration
	Geography has the ability to stimulate a deep level of curiosity and fascination about the physical and human world, whilst also encouraging a deeper moral outlook and intellectual understanding of the environment		Studying the significance of speeches and other forms of communication as historical sources can help bring numerous virtues into focus. For example, Winston Churchill's 'We shall fight on the beaches' speech from 4 June 1940 (see the Teaching Character through the Primary Curriculum character education resources[a]) facilitates discussions on resilience, honesty, leadership, and service
			When exploring human geography, such as types of settlement, economic activity, and the distribution of natural resources, pupils will often contrast their lives to the lives of others. Pupils are encouraged to think critically, to reflect, and to demonstrate compassion and empathy for others
	In Citizenship/Social Studies lessons, pupils learn more than simply knowing about political systems and structures. Pupils are challenged to be active citizens, practising and reflecting on the issues they have explored in the classroom within their communities		Pupils may be involved in learning about an issue in their local environment, participating in decision-making processes to engage with opinions of a range of stakeholders from their community
			Exploring the roles of public institutions and voluntary groups in society, and the ways in which citizens work together to improve their communities, enables pupils to demonstrate numerous civic virtues, including service and volunteering

Subject area/ subjects	Key connections	Example virtues in focus	Elaboration
Literature	It would be possible to find examples of almost all of the virtues through the themes of literature and many of the virtues can be seamlessly included in Literature curriculums via writing, reading, or drama exercises Literature often includes numerous implicit and explicit virtues, providing a multitude of opportunities to discuss and reflect on characters' virtues, vices, and use of practical wisdom (or lack thereof)	civility compassion courage creativity determination humility justice kindness perseverance self-regulation service	Studying seminal texts (see the *Knightly Virtues* character education resources, for example[b]) typically focuses pupils on the virtues of self-regulation, humility, and justice. Texts offer clear scope for exploration of different points of view through the appreciation of deeply complex and morally variable situations Poetry is also a great vehicle for the exploration of character and virtues. Poetry written during the First World War, such as *Dulce Et Decorum Est* by Wilfred Owen (see the *Virtue, Vice and Verse* character education resources[c]), provides an avenue for exploring the virtues of courage, justice, and integrity For younger pupils, picture books (see the *Read, Grow, Go* character education resources[d]) can be used to discuss and reflect on a range of virtues, such as kindness, compassion, and honesty

(continued)

Table 5.1 (continued)

Subject area/ subjects	Key connections	Example virtues in focus	Elaboration
Mathematics	When initially thinking about character education opportunities in Mathematics, non-specialists tend to think immediately about the development of performance virtues, especially when pupils face challenges in their understanding of key mathematical concepts and skills When explored in depth, the Mathematics curriculum provides a wealth of other opportunities to discuss and reflect upon virtues, in particular when everyday applications (when investigating data and statistics, for example) are involved	compassion critical thinking curiosity determination fairness honesty perseverance resourcefulness teamwork	When teaching data handling, pupils begin with interpretations of bar charts and graphs and progress to more detailed analytical interpretations. Within these lessons, the right questioning can develop pupils' understanding of fairness, as well curiosity and resourcefulness When studying algebra, pupils will investigate number patterns and number puzzles encouraging problem-solving, critical thinking, and determination The applied contexts in which pupils learn about numbers and descriptive statistics can help pupils to develop a compassionate understanding of others' situations and needs – for example, when using statistics to understand and describe poverty, food shortages, and employment
Modern Languages	Modern Language curriculums not only provide pupils with the ability to learn the grammar and vocabulary of new languages but to explore the cultures of other countries, developing their intercultural understanding Modern Languages provide pupils with experiences outside of their own lives and can be a significant vehicle for the delivery of character education	civility communication confidence curiosity empathy respect	When learning a language, pupils can be encouraged to foster a curiosity and deeper understanding of countries, cultures, and other people, in the process developing an empathic and respectful disposition Learning to communicate orally in a new language requires developing confidence, so that pupils can communicate effectively and learn from and with others

Subject area/ subjects	Key connections	Example virtues in focus	Elaboration
Physical Education	Physical Education explicitly teaches a variety of virtues, and these are often central to the subject. Character-based work in Physical Education requires that teachers are not just good sports coaches but also good character coaches. Included within this is modelling good character to pupils	communication confidence courage fairness humility integrity leadership reflection self-discipline teamwork	When developing a range of tactics and strategies to use in competitive games, pupils can be taught about the importance of fair play via the virtues of humility, fairness, and integrity. Through reflection on their conduct and performance, pupils can evaluate their virtues across a range of activities
Personal, Social, Health, and Economic Education	Forms of Personal, Social, Health, and Economic Education (which often come under a range of guises) can be seen as a natural partner to character education as they are specifically focused on the personal development of pupils – helping them learn how to live as human beings and as members of society	All virtues	Forms of Personal, Social, Health, and Economic Education can be planned so that the virtues become the driving force behind the curriculum. For example, in a primary school the virtues of self-control, perseverance, or confidence could drive topics of keeping healthy and exercising. Likewise, in secondary schools the virtues of community awareness, respect, and justice could be used to frame relationships with others in the community

(continued)

Table 5.1 (continued)

Subject area/subjects	Key connections	Example virtues in focus	Elaboration
Sciences	The Science curriculum provides pupils with key knowledge, understanding, and skills necessary for scientific enquiry but also lends itself directly to character education Science has a fundamental concern for the truth which is established through an ethical understanding of scientific knowledge and practice. The curriculum also provides opportunities for pupils to engage with, explore, and understand underlying ethical issues	compassion creativity critical thinking curiosity determination honesty integrity justice perseverance resourcefulness	When designing an experiment, pupils must ensure they have planned for a fair test and when evaluating their findings, they must display honesty and integrity to showcase their findings Pupils should acquire the scientific knowledge to understand the uses and implications of science, today and for the future, and in doing so need to be provided opportunities to discuss ethical issues connected with the practice of science, such as animal testing and clinical drug trials

a https://www.jubileecentre.ac.uk/1709/character-education/teacher-resources/teaching-character-primary
b https://www.jubileecentre.ac.uk/1641/character-education
c https://www.jubileecentre.ac.uk/1725/character-education
d https://www.jubileecentre.ac.uk/2925/character-education/teacher-resources/read-grow-go

Case Study 5.4: Character Education through Personal, Social, Health, and Economic Education

BEN MILLER, House Tutor, Head of Theology and Philosophy, Reading School, Reading, UK

At Reading School, character education is an integral part of the school curriculum and wider school culture. Character education is embedded into the main school curriculum, as well as being taught through its Personal, Social, Health, and Economic (PSHE) education and 'Floreat' character education provision. This curriculum time gives pupils the opportunity to explore issues within key PSHE, Sex and Relationships Education, and Spiritual, Moral, Social, and Cultural development topics through 'the lens' of character and virtues. This approach to character education allows the curriculum to explore important issues from the perspective of the character development of the pupils. Looking at the virtues in the context of issues also allows greater exploration of how different virtues might interact or collide in real life. In this approach, virtues are rarely encountered individually, allowing pupils to reason and apply the virtues to situations that they might encounter.

Reading School believes that character education is the responsibility of all staff who have contact with children and young people. In the school, virtues are caught through the culture, ethos, and positive example of school staff. Virtues are also taught explicitly through educational experiences that equip pupils with the language, knowledge, understanding, skills, and attributes that enable character development. Finally, Reading School seeks to provide opportunities that support pupils to seek, desire, and freely pursue their own character development.

Content of the Reading School Character Curriculum

The character education provision taught through PSHE has been developed by teachers and draws on a neo-Aristotelian approach to character and virtue and the extensive research and work of the Jubilee Centre for Character and Virtues. There is an introductory module, aimed at Key Stage 3 (Years 7–9) pupils on the philosophy of virtue ethics, which gives pupils the vocabulary of virtue and an understanding of the process of character and virtue development. This module explains the philosophical underpinning of Reading School's approach to character education. Subsequent lessons, which focus on different topics, fall under four broad headings: flourishing individuals, flourishing relationships, digital flourishing, and flourishing societies. Examples of the topics that appear under each heading are shown below.

Many of the topics, including heathy relationships and online safety, are introduced in Key Stage 3 and re-visited in Key Stage 4 (Years 10 and 11). Within each topic pupils have the opportunity to use a range of tools to reflect on their character. These include: moral dilemmas, the biographies of role models, and reflection opportunities linked to serving the local community.

Flourishing individuals	Flourishing relationships	Digital flourishing	Societal flourishing
Healthy eating	Friendships	Wise use of technology	Communities
Exercise	Family relationships	Cyber bullying	Volunteering
Harmful substances	Peer pressure	Fake news	Careers
Emotional health	Managing conflict	Online relationships	Democracy

Structure of the curriculum

The curriculum is divided into resources for each year group from Year 7 to Year 13. There are a series of detailed lesson plans and photocopiable resources for staff to use with each year group. In Key Stage 3 there are also presentations available for each lesson. Within each year group, there are four topic areas and each topic area contains two or three lessons. Each weekly lesson in Key Stage 3 and Key Stage 4 is designed to last approximately one hour.

Staff at Reading School enjoy this unique approach to teaching character education through PSHE and using character as a lens through which to explore issues. In adopting this approach, staff are able to be flexible in their delivery and set the important issues, such as managing conflict, online safety, and healthy relationships, in the context of character development – ensuring pupils are reflecting on the kind of person they are and the kind of person they are becoming.

The wider curriculum

In the previous section, we examined ways character can be, and is, taught through core subjects and subject areas. As we suggested earlier in the chapter, however, the curriculum within schools – and by extension aspects of character taught – run wider than these. In this final section of the chapter, we outline some other prominent ways that character can be taught within the daily life of schools.

Form/home groups and assemblies

Creativity is the key for schools who are committed to teaching character but are unable to find space within their subject curriculum or who wish to extend the teaching of character through subjects. Many secondary schools have found great value in including character education as a structured part of the daily form/home groups. Although what constitutes form/home time varies from school to school, traditionally it is a set period of time (usually 20–30 minutes) in the morning and/or afternoon where pupils register for school and discuss progress with their form or home tutor. The regular frequency of form time and the relationship that builds between the form/home tutor and pupils provides a valuable platform for character education. As Case Study 5.5 highlights, form time can be used to incorporate a modified character education curriculum in which a series of short lessons can be built upon over a week or longer period of time.

Case Study 5.5: Character-Focused Form Time

DR TOM HARRISON, Reader in Character Education Pedagogy and Practice, Director of Education, Jubilee Centre for Character and Virtues, School of Education, University of Birmingham, UK

I completed my GSCEs at my secondary school about thirty years ago. I still remember a great deal from my five years at the school; friends of course, some of the teachers, and even some of the lessons. One thing I can't remember is what we did during the form time that was held each morning. This twenty minutes, if I remember rightly, was dedicated to taking the register and chatting with my friends. In total, tutorial time took up sixty hours of each of my secondary school years. That's a lot of tutor time, with not much to show (or at least remember!) for it.

I know this is not the situation in many schools today, where form or home time is seen as an opportunity to develop the character of pupils. In these schools, form time is focused on developing qualities that will have a positive impact on attainment, behaviour, and employability, as well as pupils' lives more generally. Given technological advancements, the traditional business of form time, such as taking the register and handing out notices, can be managed electronically. This leaves more time for a focus on personal development. It is a time for form tutors to really get to know about the character qualities, as opposed to the academic abilities, of the pupils in their care. It is a time, every day, when form tutors can help pupils understand what character is and why it matters. It is a time to explicitly try to build a language of character that all pupils share and can use throughout the school day. It is a time to encourage pupils to reflect on the dilemmas that they experience in and out of school – dilemmas that require them to show character. It is a chance to learn from real-life stories – to learn about what virtues are present when things go well in a pupil's life, as well as what virtues and qualities are required to bounce back when they haven't gone so well.

I do not think there is a blueprint for how character-focused tutor time should be run. In fact, it is probably best not to have too much structure so that form tutors have the space to respond to the character issues of the day – be they in the news and/or linked to the lives of pupils. However, some structure is needed. For example, teachers might use a reflective journal such as the ones developed in the *My Character*[1] programme, which focuses on future-mindedness.

The journal follows a structure for each of the virtues associated with being future-minded. It starts with inspiration (normally in the form of a role model), then an activity that develops pupils' knowledge about the virtue and concludes with a piece of reflective writing. Activities that develop virtue literacy in pupils can be used to bring some structure to tutorial times. I know some schools also encourage daily reflections every morning.

An explicit focus on character during tutorial times will not be enough on its own. Character education should be a whole-school endeavour and woven into every part of the school day – like a stick of rock. However, tutorial time is an ideal chance to remind pupils, every day, what character is and why it matters.

School assemblies also provide teachers with opportunities to incorporate character education on a regular basis. In most schools, assemblies occur at least once a week and involve the gathering of different year groups who engage with teachers and invited speakers. Within assemblies, at both the primary and secondary school level, pupils are told stories, listen to presentations and music, and are given opportunities to reflect on the content of the messages conveyed. It is common for schools and teachers to use assemblies to teach about character and virtues – even in schools where the terms *character* and *virtue* are not used explicitly. For example, the content of stories told in assemblies often touch on, or are directly focused on, good character and behaviour. Assemblies therefore provide teachers with natural as well as regular opportunities to consciously teach about character. In Chapter 7, we provide links to resources and websites that include examples of assemblies alongside other taught approaches. We encourage you to engage with these examples and to consider how assembly time might be used as part of a planned approach to teaching character.

Enrichment

All schools offer extra-curricular activities. These activities, which include sports clubs, social action opportunities, outdoor learning, and a range of other activities, give pupils the opportunities to develop and express particular interests, broadening and extending the more formal curriculum. A growing number of schools are recognising the value of extra-curricular activities as part of their character education provision. This has led some schools to re-evaluate how they deliver extra-curricular activities, and to rename this provision as *enrichment*. For these schools, enrichment is not strictly speaking *extra*-curricular, as it forms a core part of the school's curriculum and ethos. A school-wide enrichment programme ensures *all* pupils have access to the widest range of experiences and learning opportunities, as highlighted in Case Study 5.6.

Case Study 5.6: Enrichment at the University of Birmingham School

REBECCA TIGUE, Head of School, University of Birmingham School, Birmingham, UK

The University of Birmingham School opened in 2015 as the UK's first secondary University Training School, as well as the first school in the UK to have been established with an explicit focus on character development at the core of its vision. Our school has worked in close partnership with the Jubilee Centre since its conception in developing its character education provision to develop a 'caught, taught, and sought' character curriculum, where character education infuses all operations at the school; across curriculum, policy, governance, and professional. Whilst we are unrelenting in our quest for academic excellence, we believe that it is our job to prepare children for 'the tests of life, not just a life of tests'; we want all members of our school – children and adults – to be engaged, fulfilled, and happy citizens, leading flourishing lives, and building better communities.

Virtue is practical; there is little benefit in knowing what is theoretically virtuous if it cannot be put in to practice, so to supplement a more theoretical taught curriculum delivered through form time, assemblies, and within subjects, the school is also committed to finding opportunities to widen the scope of what pupils can experience by having an enrichment programme built into an extended school week. Whilst most schools do their very best to offer a rich variety of after-school clubs, the 'opt in' nature often means they are run by a small cohort of keen and dedicated staff, and attended by those pupils who are already confident, curious, or self-disciplined, and who appreciate and enjoy the benefits of a rich extra-curricular life. Our ambitiously inclusive programme ensures all pupils (and all staff) are fully immersed in the enrichment experience.

The enrichment experience itself has two strands: a two-hour project-based strand, which all pupils take part in, and a one-hour 'elective' strand, which offers different activities for the pupils to opt in to.

The first strand enables all pupils to rotate around a series of experiences that span the four 'building blocks of character', encouraging pupils to consider the intellectual, moral, civic, and performance virtues. The development of character is the foundation upon which the first strand of our enrichment programme is built; every enrichment activity is considered carefully and explicit links to the development of character are made.

We are a diverse school with a unique nodal admissions policy, which means our pupils come from all corners of the city of Birmingham. The Year 7 projects are therefore based around the theme 'Our Community', where pupils begin to truly discover their city and the communities within it. For example, we work with a local arts organisation who explore different parts of the city with a class at a time and then provide opportunities to develop curiosity and creativity by creating a newspaper of poetry, photography, and art reflecting the communities they have visited. The 'Thank You Café' project is an opportunity for pupils to express their gratitude to friends and family and for the community to come together as pupils prepare, cook, and serve a three-course meal, which they then invite their guests to come and enjoy together. The Year 7 projects also include a social action project where pupils begin to learn the double benefit of helping others – ranging from packing bags in the local supermarket to fishing shopping trolleys out of the local canal – and a series of visits to our university to inspire future-mindedness.

In Year 9, the project strand is used to ensure all pupils have the opportunity to complete their Duke of Edinburgh Bronze Award. This is a big commitment of time and money, but one which we feel is totally worthwhile. Nothing builds character quite like a D of E expedition.

The second strand of enrichment is possible because every member of staff – both teaching staff and support staff – is committed to offering enrichment opportunities that they are passionate about. This gives every pupil a wide range of activities to choose from for an hour a week, for six weeks at a time. Pupils can choose from jogging to journalism, cooking to kick-boxing, or set up a club themselves if they can find a member of staff who will run it. The enrichment provision is designed to give pupils experiences that they may not otherwise seek out, learn from being with pupils they would not normally meet, and see staff in a totally different way. There is nothing like realising your rugby coach is also a keen knitter!

Overall, an enrichment programme like ours is a huge commitment to undertake. Logistically, planning what are effectively new timetables every six weeks requires admin support and a lot of staff goodwill, and the extended school week means staff and pupils really have to practise resilience to get them through to period 5 on a Friday. But if we genuinely want to create spaces where children feel loved, safe, happy, and are able to flourish, the hard work is worth it.

Learning through enrichment activities affords pupils opportunities to experiment, to try new things, and to learn from their mistakes. A well-developed enrichment programme enables and encourages pupils to discover new passions, develop new interests, and build new skills. This said, it cannot be assumed that pupils will automatically develop character just by engaging in enrichment activities. Rather, and like other processes that support pupils' character development, the outcomes of enrichment activities need to be made explicit, connecting to the ethos and culture of the school, and providing space for discussion and reflection. In the next chapter, we delve deeper into these outcomes, focusing on social action.

Conclusion

In this chapter, you have been introduced to the various ways that character can be taught within, through, and across the curriculums that exist in schools.

Whether in formal subject curriculums or through the wide range of curriculums that exist within enrichment programmes and activities, these taught elements of character enable pupils to learn about, understand, analyse, and evaluate the meaning of virtues through a number of lenses and perspectives. Through this direct engagement with character and virtues, pupils explore key components of virtue, connecting these to their own lives and to their developing understanding of core subject content, concepts, and skills.

Note

1   https://www.jubileecentre.ac.uk/1631/character-education/teacher-resources/my-character

Further reading

Arthur, J., Harrison, T., and Wright, D. (2016) *Teaching Character through the Curriculum*. Birmingham: University of Birmingham, Jubilee Centre for Character and Virtues. [Online.] Available at: https://www.jubileecentre.ac.uk/userfiles/jubileecentre/pdf/TeachingCharacterThroughtheCurriculum.pdf
This guide was produced in collaboration with teachers working to develop character through subjects in their school. It provides practical examples and approaches to including character virtues in the subject curriculum.

Character.org, *Promising Practices*. Available at: https://www.character.org/promising-practices
Web-based pages from Character.org which provide real-life examples from schools in the US, including how schools have incorporated character in their curriculums.

Harrison, T., Bawden, M., and Rogerson, L. (2016) *Teaching Character Through Subjects: Educating the Virtues through and within 14 Secondary Subjects*. Birmingham: University of Birmingham, Jubilee Centre for Character and Virtues. [Online.] Available at: http://www.jubileecentre.ac.uk/1676/character-education/resources/teaching-characterthrough-subjects
Funded by the Department for Education (DfE) in England, the Teaching Character Through Subjects project worked with 29 teachers from 28 schools to create an innovative resource for building character within 14 subjects across the school curriculum.

6 Character education beyond the school gates through social action

Introduction

While much of the formal character education pupils receive takes place within the confines of the school, the extent to which community-based activities can support the development of character remains of central interest to research and practice in the field. Engagement with and within community settings enables pupils to both express and develop their character. Indeed, social action – sometimes also referred to as service-learning – is a core pedagogical strategy for character education (Berkowitz and Bier, 2005). Providing pupils with opportunities for moral action is one of the *11 Principles of Effective Character Education* detailed by Character.org and to which you were introduced in Chapter 1.[1] The principle proposes that 'through meaningful experiences and reflection opportunities, schools with a culture of character help pupils develop their commitment to being honest and trustworthy, to volunteer their time and talents to the common good, and when necessary, to show the courage to stand up for what is right'. Undertaking well-planned and implemented youth social action offers pupils the opportunity to practise and gain real-life skills and experiences, fostering meaningful relationships with others. Crucially, the focus of social action is not only on learning in the community or on learning about the community, but on addressing and seeking to impact positively on appropriate issues and needs.

Although research and practice on social action typically focuses on the broad category of 'youth', more recently there has been a growing focus on the extent to which social action might form part of effective character education for younger children as well. Following this introduction, in the first section of this chapter we consider key definitions of, and approaches to, social action as a core mechanism for character education across the primary and secondary ages. We also detail some of the key educational benefits of engaging pupils in social action. In the second section, we address core principles that educators should consider in planning social action experiences for pupils. After setting out these core principles, we also consider the benefits of working with community partners to develop social action opportunities, as well as the importance of building bridges between practices within the school and social action experiences beyond the school.

In ending this introduction, one final comment that should underpin building social action remains; namely, that how young people approach and conceive the various forms of social action will not necessarily be uniform and, equally significantly, may well differ from the understandings held by adults (Arthur et al., 2015a). This point is eloquently expressed by Body et al. (2020) in their work on charitable giving with children of primary school age. They argue that rather than viewing charitable giving as being concerned with raising more money, children adopt a different stance, focusing instead on 'acts of everyday kindness'. For these children, charity is 'an embodiment of a set of behaviours, actions and values that are rooted in ideas of kindness, fairness and empathy – the building blocks of social justice and democracy'.

The view expressed by Body et al. in this passage reminds us that it can be the case that pupils may already approach the various forms of social action from a character-based (or at least a values-based) perspective. Given that children are already involved in a range of social action activities (whether volunteering, fundraising, making donations, or other forms), as you progress through the chapter it is also worth reflecting upon the diverse understandings and experiences pupils bring with them to, and beyond, the classroom.

Chapter Objectives

By the end of this chapter, you should have:

- Considered key definitions of social action and the role that social action can play in developing character
- Examined key pedagogical approaches to, and questions about, developing social action programmes in schools
- Reflected on real-life examples of social action to consider how you will approach your own practice in this area.

What is social action?

One of the first challenges teachers may face in approaching social action is to arrive at a general understanding of what social action constitutes and implies. This first task is not helped by the fact that a number of terms are used (whether as direct synonyms or close relations) for what we in this chapter call 'social action'. These terms include, amongst others, community involvement, civic engagement, youth activism, experiential learning, and active citizenship. A useful and important starting point in trying to pinpoint more clearly what social action is and involves has developed in the context of significant policy interest in, and practical application of, 'youth social action' in the UK. The definition established by The Campaign for Youth Social Action (2013: 6) in 2013 framed social action as: 'Young people taking practical action in the service of others in order to create positive social change that is of benefit to the wider community as well as to the young person themselves'. The #*iwill* campaign has expanded upon this definition, casting social action as encompassing 'activities that young people do to make a positive difference to others or the environment'.[2]

The 2019 #*iwill* impact report[3] sets out seven 'forms' of youth social action, indicating the breadth of activities that can fall under this banner:

- volunteering
- fundraising for a charity
- being a mentor, tutor, leader, or coach
- being on a school council
- helping out a neighbour who needs support
- taking care of animals or the environment
- campaigning on an issue that you care about.

As you can see from reading this list – and from the activities in Fig. 6.1 – social action can involve activities that: are school-based and/or community-based; focus on a short-term and/or long-term needs; concentrate on humans, animals,

Figure 6.1 The breadth of social action

and/or the environment; can be local, national, and/or global in scope; and involve the social and/or the political to different extents.

In other contexts – most notably the US – the concept and practice of 'service-learning' is preferred to the term 'social action'. The seminal definition of service-learning is provided by Eyler and Giles (1999: 7–8) in their book *Where's the Learning in Service-Learning*: 'Service-learning is a form of experiential education … [in which] learning occurs through a cycle of action and reflection … Experience enhances understanding; understanding leads to more effective action'. Through the process of service-learning, pupils work together with others in their communities to bring together intellectual commitment, moral direction, and political understanding to focus on community-based issues – and to do so in reflective and reflexive ways. Social action is constituted by ongoing processes of action, reflection, communication, and negotiation (Wildemeersch, 2009), and serves to connect pupils' character development with their formation as citizens. In this sense, service-learning/social action is fundamentally concerned with integrating and balancing *personal development* with *community development*. As such, service-learning is based on a range of experiential pedagogical theories located across the work of John Dewey and David Kolb, amongst others.

A now large body of research has pointed to the personal, educational, and societal benefits of pupils' engagement in social action (Arthur et al., 2015a, 2017b; Bernacki and Bernt, 2007; Body and Hogg, 2019; Hart, 2007; Hogg, 2016). Hecht (2003: 28) has illustrated the potential benefits of service-learning in the following, general terms:

> Service-learning enriches a pupil's world, providing new experiences and challenges. Through planning, service and reflection, pupils are encouraged to examine the tasks at hand, to develop plans for dealing with the obvious and unexpected, to take action, and to consider how these actions are understandable given other academic and life knowledge.

As Thompson and Metcalfe (2020) have pointed out, while 'there is a growing body of research that articulates the links between participation in YSA [youth social action] and character development', it remains the case that the actual 'types of character strength that are built, or valued, by those doing YSA are less well understood' (see Birdwell et al., 2013; Taylor-Collins et al., 2019; Lamb et al., 2019). Their analysis of the self-reported character strengths of 300 #iwill Ambassadors across six cohorts (2014–2019), with strengths chosen from a predetermined list presented to them by *Step Up to Serve*, found that '"confidence" and "community awareness" consistently appeared in the top five strengths identified by respondents, regardless of cohort'. In addition, '"Leadership" and "communication" appeared in the top five from 2015 onwards'. Overall, across the cohorts performance virtues were the most prevalent, though they note that a consistent reporting of 'community awareness' within the top five character strengths from 2015 onwards suggests recognition of the civic dimension. These strengths, while self-reported, point to the personal and inter-personal qualities social action builds. Of course, it may not be possible or desirable to cover a wide range of virtues within a particular instance of social action. This said, it is nevertheless crucial that school leaders and teachers are intentional and explicit about which dispositions are being developed, including how these are understood by those involved (teachers, pupils, community partners, and so on).

Case Study 6.1: Social Action Beyond the Classroom

CAROLE JONES, Headteacher, Yeading Junior School, Hayes, UK

Character development is evident in all aspects of school life and learning at Yeading Junior School; it is at the very heart of our school's ethos. Empowering our children and giving them a voice in school and in other spaces has enabled our children to influence others for the good. The benefits of this empowerment, voice, and influence are visible in pupils' academic performance and in their awareness of the importance of making good choices. With regard to the latter, character education has enhanced the children's perception of the need to reflect and learn from the decisions they and others make.

At Yeading Junior School, character development is caught, taught, and sought. The knowledge and skills that emerge through our work are shared with others at home through a range of communications and actions as well as by the children as advocates themselves. Harnessing families to support character education in the school has further embedded and strengthened our work. Issues are explored through the curriculum, whether formally or informally. These issues are brought forward by the children through their learning or have been brought to their attention by others, creating opportunities that both empower and enliven thinking and establishing platforms and opportunities that enable children to discuss and debate at a mature level.

Providing an abundance of enrichment activities and numerous opportunities to take part in social action has enhanced our innovative approach to character education. Social action projects and activities developed within school provide a vehicle for children to deepen their understanding of the school's set of virtues – that are known and shared by all within school, embraced by families, and recognised further afield. Social action at Yeading Junior School is borne out of the children's strong desire to make a difference. Social action may be school-based or involve activities beyond the school, and could involve a class, group, or the whole school. The key for us is to share and promote the action across the whole school. Indeed, social action forms a well-established part of the culture of the school.

The establishment of links with a range of external social action providers has enabled the development of partnerships and networks, which in turn make it easier to provide opportunities for our young learners to explore, act upon, and learn about character education through social action. Leadership roles established amongst the children have driven many of these social action activities and projects forward. These leadership roles have also enabled all children to understand the importance of teamwork and how it can positively influence the whole community. Our student leaders often work with younger children to research social action projects, work on actions independently, and subsequently plan the action. Our wide-ranging enrichment activities and our commitment to social action have had a tangible impact on the school community.

Social action activities present children with a wide range of opportunities. A notable one of these involves children taking an active role in an intergenerational project with a neighbouring 'live at home' scheme. Children were able to develop their own skills whilst enhancing those of others through assisting in delivering iPad training to members of the scheme. They have also learned from the wisdom of the elderly and explored the impact of loneliness whilst reflecting upon the importance of positive interactions with others. Another social action project engaged learners in designing and creating survival kits for the homeless and inspiring staff to volunteer at a local soup kitchen. Our student leaders have effectively led projects on the environment and climate change, which have also included planting trees within the local community. The school has also worked closely with other neighbouring schools to raise awareness of global issues through local campaigns, such as one around providing clean water.

At Yeading we pride ourselves on the fact we have many social action opportunities available within the school, enabling children to use a range of transferrable learning skills whilst also demonstrating a deep understanding of our character virtues. Within the local community, our children have become known for their skill, determination, and compassion and we think the opportunities we provide them with will encourage them to continue engaging with social action as they get older.

Case Study 6.1 illustrates a number of the points we have set out so far in this chapter; it also highlights that at the bedrock of effective and meaningful social action is *critical reflection*, without which action may be misinformed, misjudged, and misdirected. Lamb et al. (2019: 136) have referred to this process as the 'dialectic of action and reflection', without which pupils would not develop 'an intelligent habit of social action'. As Body et al. (2020) argue, we should use these opportunities to help children challenge and come to their own views of charity and associated virtues, rather than simply training them to be 'good citizens'. Here the words of John Dewey (1933: 9), written nearly a century ago, remain pertinent. On his understanding, reflection consists of the 'active, persistent and careful consideration of any belief or supposed form of knowledge in the light of grounds that support it and further conclusions to which it tends'.

The 'double-benefit'

As mentioned above, at the heart of social action is the integration and balance of personal development and community development. This recognition is the basis of 'the double benefit' – a tool that has been developed to help those involved in social action, including educators and young people themselves, to consider both personal and community development. The double benefit is constituted by the processes through which social action:

> develops a range of capacities in young people, while simultaneously building and enhancing the communities with which young people engage. The process is one through which young people connect with issues they feel passionately about and which affect others, bringing people from different backgrounds and communities together. In planning to have a positive impact on others and taking action, young people work collaboratively to make an important contribution to society while at the same time building their own self-worth and sense of belonging – capacities essential to human and societal flourishing. This double benefit is central to character development. (Jubilee Centre, 2014: 2)

Any educator seeking to develop new social action experiences or reflecting on existing opportunities will immediately appreciate the need to tread carefully and clearly across what remains complex and contested ground. Not least, it remains the case – and this echoes wider research on volunteering and philanthropy – that the reasons why young people become involved in youth social action are likely not only to be varied but may also differ from the reasons that sustain their motivation. Either way, such reasons and motivations are likely to straddle the personal and the communal. In addition, the focus on the more instrumental elements of the personal benefits may have important educational benefits necessary to move pupils towards more settled intrinsic motivations. Lamb et al. (2019: 138–139) explain that:

> On an Aristotelian approach, offering recognition to those who excel in social action or demonstrate impressive commitment and character serves several educational functions. For example, it provides youth with access to role models to emulate and motivates them to perform similar actions, even if initially for the sake of recognition. Eventually, as participants see the value of benefitting their community and developing their character, they may be less motivated by awards and recognition. They may even find pleasure in performing social action and thereby act with the characteristic ease that follows from possessing a virtue.

It is also useful to consider further dimensions within each 'side' of the double benefit. With regard to the individual benefit, we might ask whether these benefits tend towards the instrumental or the intrinsic. Here David Brooks' (2016) distinction between 'résumé' and 'eulogy' virtues introduced in Chapter 1 is again relevant. This way of viewing the individual benefit is useful for reflecting on how engagement in youth social action in educational settings can be framed (either separately or at the same time) as adding to the individual's career capital (i.e. experiences and skills that make them more employable and that 'look good on the CV'), and developing dispositions and virtues that are more deep-rooted and intrinsically worthwhile (those, for example, that develop the moral, intellectual, and civic character of the pupil).

Moving to the community/societal benefit, we can ask whether the benefit is short-term or long-term. Of course, in everyday reality pupils' engagement in social action may be focused on both short-term and long-term needs/benefits. However, it is useful for those involved in social action to reflect on the extent to which pupils, in addition to working towards more immediate community benefit, are provided with the opportunity to move to involvement in longer-term, sustainable actions and commitments. While not necessarily 'in tension', without the opportunity to engage in action aimed at long-term, structural benefit, pupils are unlikely to develop the deep relationships – and indeed change – fundamental to building the character of themselves, their peers, and their wider communities. Of course, some of the social action pupils engage with may be rather limited in scope, such as when they make a one-off donation in order to forgo wearing school uniform for the day. These stand-alone instances have some value. However, as Lamb et al. (2019: 135) suggest, 'to reflect a virtuous habit, social action must constitute an ongoing practice, not merely a one-off experience'.

The educational point being made here was eloquently expressed by a senior leader in an Australian secondary school in an interview with one of the authors, in which the leader critically reflected on some of the social action experiences pupils at the school were engaged in:

> For us to get involved we've got to have community partners – and our community partners are either local or international. For us to get involved in them there has to be the following things. There's got to be an educational component, our pupils have to come out of it – they have to learn, they're here to learn, not to learn how to run barbecues or whatever it is for fundraising in there. There's got to be an educational element to it as well. Then there has to be pupil involvement in the whole process which means most of our projects come from pupils. We also believe there has to be some sort of timeframe for the involvement and usually the timeframe will be five years. We are not going to say 'well this year we'll do this, well next year let's do that'. If we commit ourselves to a partner, it's a five year partnership which has set goals. The aim should be to try and achieve sustainability in that project and have an end – if we have an end point in there. And then fourthly it needs to be pupil-managed as well. Usually we will have a pupil project manager who will run the project from our end. Only then do we get involved in fundraising for that project.

As this senior leader observes, social action is at its most meaningful when it incorporates critical intellectual virtues, including curiosity and reflection, in order to challenge preconceptions and to ensure that opportunities for shared learning and understanding (of core issues, of interests, and of others) remain at the heart of social action. The very articulation of a pupil's own views, for example, builds a certain level of reflexivity when these views come into contact with those of others, enabling pupils to discuss, hear, and listen. An apt example that illustrates how engaging in social action can build virtue literacy is provided by Wimborne (2020), who quotes a Year 4 (8–9-year-old) pupil involved in the RSA4[4] programme: '[B]efore I thought working as a team is just doing work together. But now I think it's like listening to each other's ideas, sharing ideas, making them better and I've learned to do what teamwork really is'.

To conclude this section, the *A Habit of Service* (Arthur et al., 2017b) study undertaken by the Jubilee Centre highlights a number of benefits of developing a habit of service in young people. Those who had made service into a habit were more likely to:

- be involved more frequently and in a wider range of service activities
- identify themselves more closely with exemplars of moral and civic virtues
- have parents/friends who are also involved in the same kinds of activities
- believe they have the time, skills, opportunity, and confidence to participate in service
- have service embedded in their school/college/university environment
- be able to reflect on their experience of service
- recognise that service brings benefits for themselves and others.

Echoing these benefits, Case Study 6.2 highlights the outcomes of service-learning and associated activities within the enrichment activities of British School Manila.

Case Study 6.2: Connecting Service-Learning, Activities, and Wellbeing

CARRIE TAYLOR, English Teacher, British School Manila, Taguig, Philippines

The British School Manila (BSM) prides itself on living its Missions and Vision Statement. This is wholeheartedly seen and felt throughout the school.

> 'The British School Manila ... provides an outstanding holistic international education for British children and English speaking children of other nationalities.'

Directly linked to character are the following statements taken from the Mission and Vision of the school.

> 'The British School Manila aims for its pupils to flourish through:
> - Being resilient in adversity
> - Application and effort
> - Meeting challenges by accepting that risk-taking and making mistakes are positive parts of learning

- Being respectful, honest and kind, have integrity and take responsibility for their own actions.'

These statements are further secured in our wellbeing framework. Through the application in and outside of the classroom, we also aim for pupils of character who are:

- 'Happy, healthy and managing their own well-being
- Confident in expressing and being themselves
- Making their world sustainable, peaceful and fair.'
  (British School Manila Mission and Vision Statement)

Outside of the taught curriculum at BSM, the school seeks to combine a range of connected activities and opportunities for pupils to develop their character. This is done significantly in the school through service-learning and activities. The wellbeing framework further provides a support structure for parent workshops, staff CPD, and school community support – including an extension on wellbeing support for staff.

Service-learning
At BSM, each year group from Year 1 to Year 10 is allocated a service-learning partner. These include local charities, schools, orphanages, and animal sanctuaries, which pupils raise funds for throughout the year. This is done by holding activities such as car washes, bake sales, resource drives and collections, shoe box appeals, online tournaments, and other sponsored activities. Once funds are raised, we hold a service-learning week in January in which BSM pupils work alongside their service-learning partners. This work has involved handing out solar-panelled lights so that people don't have to use kerosene lamps, speaking to the local communities; releasing turtle hatchlings; working and playing with children in schools and orphanages; building, painting, and planting to improve the landscape and facilities – both for our local community and those further afield. BSM has its own sustainable garden, stingless bees, and a rice terrace, and has built community housing for the blind and elderly.

Our pupils recognize they are in a fortunate and privileged position to help others in a country which is classed as 'newly industrialized'. During the service-learning week, a leader will provide a reflection space in which pupils talk about challenges they have faced and acknowledge what they are grateful for. It is an opportunity to give back, to grow and develop character traits in our pupils linked to citizenship, community, persistence, resilience, teamwork, humility, and reflection.

These activities are built upon and extended when pupils move into their International Baccalaureate years in which Creativity, Activity, Service (CAS) is a core element. Pupils work in groups and actively seek to find their own project to improve the quality of life in a community. This has included building chicken coops so that a community has a sustainable food supply, creating hydroponic watering systems for gardens, and building rooftop gardens on a local hospital roof. There are approximately sixteen projects each year, and these have a lasting impact on the communities the pupils support. Many pupils go beyond this group project, setting up their own charities: from making clay earrings to support treatment for street cats, to clothing brands which support indigenous weavers, and most recently a drive with pupils making PPE resources for front line workers. The impact on our pupils is also noteworthy – they are kind, resourceful, compassionate, conscientious, and motivated to make positive change to their world.

Activities week
In June, senior school pupils are taken out of their comfort zone for activities week. They may have to camp on a beach, sleep in the jungle in a hammock, trek for 6–10 hours a day through the mountains, go canyoning or white water rafting. They often won't have access to electricity or showers. One particular trip used discussion, journaling, and self-reporting to go alongside the experience. There were three phases to this trip: pre-trip, during-journaling, and post-trip. Pupils considered and wrote responses to the following:

Pre-trip meeting

What anxieties do you have about our trip? Address what you are thinking and what you are feeling.

What are your areas of personal strength? What are you looking forward to bringing to the team?

What are your friend's (or person at the side of you) strengths? How will they help you with your concerns?

What are you keen to improve over the coming weeks? What do you anticipate gaining from the trip?

What do you expect to be your highlight? What are you most looking forward to?

During the trip Journaling

How did you struggle/fail today?

How and when were you kind today?

How were you stretched today? How did you manage this?

What are you grateful for today?

What positive aspect have you noticed about someone else today?

Post-trip reflection and reporting to parents

What did you most enjoy about your trip?

Explain how not having access to the internet has made you reflect on your relationship with social media.

Was there a time when you were stressed or when you faced adversity? Explain how you had to work with your feelings and thoughts.

Explain how you worked together with your peers to overcome challenge.

Giving pupils this opportunity to be brave and courageous and to offer them a different perspective, allows pupils once again to reflect on their character strengths. Taking them out of their comfort zone – to stretch their abilities and the boundaries they often impose on themselves – allows pupils to take risks and learn and grow in different ways to a classroom setting. The trips, journaling, and reflections help pupils to develop character and confidence, determination, resilience, gratitude, and reflection.

Planning social action experiences

So far in this chapter, you have been introduced to key definitions of social action and have been provided with an overview of some of the core benefits engagement in social action can have for pupils' personal and social development – including the cultivation of character. In this section, we turn to some core questions and ideas that should underpin the *planning* of social action experiences.

Various principles or guides exist that can help schools and teachers to develop effective social action experiences for their pupils. The *Campaign for Youth Social Action*, for example, have developed the following set of six principles which characterise 'great youth social action':

- Challenging: Stretching and engaging, as well as exciting and enjoyable.
- Youth-led: Led, owned and shaped by young people.
- Socially impactful: Creating positive social change that is of benefit to the wider community as well as to the young people themselves.
- Progressive: Progressing to other programmes and activities.
- Embedded: Becoming the norm in a young person journey towards adult and a habit for life.
- Reflective: Valuing reflection, recognition and reward.

(The Campaign for Youth Social Action, 2013: 6)

> **Reflective Activity 6.1: The Six Principles of 'great youth social action'**
>
> Find several examples of youth social action in educational settings with which you are familiar. These might be several examples from one school or could be examples from across several schools. Find out as much as you can about the examples. Next consider the examples in relation to each of the six principles of 'great youth social action'. Where do the strengths of the social action examples you have found lie? Are there any principles that could be developed further? What educational benefits might such development lead to?

The six principles above find support in wider research on social action. Studies, for example, suggest that the earlier young people begin to get involved in service, the more likely it is that service becomes a habit and also that a supportive context in which meaningful relationships are developed can serve to sustain and further engagement in social action (Arthur et al., 2017b; Body and Hogg, 2019; Taylor-Collins et al., 2019). These studies also highlight the importance of leaning from and developing pupils' vocabulary in this space. Taylor-Collins and colleagues' (2019) research showed that those with sustained engagement in youth social action had greater familiarity and closer identification with all virtues – although particularly with moral and civic virtues – and were more likely to say that their friends would appreciate people possessing those virtues.

In a survey of international literature, Davies et al. (2019: 13–16) draw out a number of pedagogical considerations and practices from theoretical and empirical studies of education for civic engagement. These include:

- A focus on real-life and relevant political questions and issues (classroom to community, local to global) and experiences that allow for the practice of different forms of civic engagement.
- Varied ways of knowing and active involvement in the learning process constructing knowledge in relation to these political questions and issues rather than simply receiving information passively.
- Opportunities to engage in enquiry-based learning – and building skills/capacities associated with enquiry.
- Collaboration and deliberative discussion.
- Building capacities for decision-making, public issue investigation, ethical thinking, peace-building, and conflict management.
- Opportunities to engage with complexity and criticality.
- Varied learning approaches and practices that are equitable and responsive to learner diversity.

Of course, school leaders and teachers face important – and at times rather challenging – decisions in developing programmes of social action for pupils.

Many of these challenges congregate around the related areas of *who initiates the social action* and *what scope that action can – and should – take*. In certain cases, social action can move into forms of activism and, when they do, tensions can arise. This is not to propose that pupil activism is, in itself, problematic; there are examples of very meaningful forms of pupil activism that work to challenge pressing social and economic inequalities (Davies et al., 2019; Seider et al., 2020). Rather, it is to suggest that educational care must be taken in thinking through and enacting pupil activism within and beyond schools. First and foremost, as educators we must reflect on our own role in shaping, directing, and – perhaps – dictating pupils' social action. Here, Roger Hart's *Ladder of Participation* remains seminal and useful. Hart (1992: 8) identifies eight rungs to the ladder. The lowest three rungs represent 'non-participation'. These are: (1) Manipulation, (2) Decoration, and (3) Tokenism. The next five rungs represent, in ascending order, 'degrees of participation'. These are: (4) Assigned but informed, (5) Consulted and informed, (6) Adult-initiated shared decisions with children, (7) Child-initiated and directed, and (8) Child-initiated shared decisions with adults. There is a clear moral dimension to teachers' work here, as can be demonstrated through Hart's ladder.

Take, for instance, the lowest rung – manipulation. When pupils are manipulated, the focus of their social action or activism is guided solely by ends determined by the educator about which pupils have no say. Manipulation is at its strongest in situations where pupils have not developed an appropriate level of critical awareness about the issues involved. In this way, pupils become ends for the teacher's own means. We can compare this manipulation with practices on the higher rungs of the ladder. In the higher rungs – those that represent 'models of genuine participation' – projects operate in a way that respect the voices and interests of young people, including their role in democratic decision-making processes. While models of genuine participation do not necessarily require teachers to be passive or to leave the initiation of projects solely to pupils, they do require teachers to place pupils' personal and social development at the very heart of social action projects. To conclude this point, and as Elizabeth Campbell (2008b: 612) reminds us, 'ethical teachers should be moral agents and moral models, not moralistic activists'.

Engaging with community partners

Schools lie at the heart of their communities and, as part of their daily activities, they will come into contact with a range of community partners. It goes without saying, therefore, that there is a wide variety of existing and potential partners that can work with schools to support and facilitate pupils' opportunities to engage in social action. These partners can range from small-scale groups that work in the local community to support a particular need or advocate for a specific issue, to large-scale, global organisations with extensive and well-developed educational programmes. In addition, a range of organisations exist that work to mediate the relationship between schools and community partners, acting as educational intermediaries to develop effective and meaningful social action.

Whether schools are working with a small local community group, a global organisation, or an educational intermediary, it is important that teachers are clear on *why* they are engaging with outside organisations. As well as wider personal and community development benefits, reasons for working with community partners include the following:

- *Experience and expertise*: Community partners widen and enhance social action though their specific and specialist knowledge of the contexts, issues, and needs involved. Sometimes this expertise will also include preparing and advising pupils for their social action.

- *Structure and connections*: Community partners can provide structure and focus to pupils' social action, helping them to gain greater insight and knowledge. Crucially, they can also make connections for pupils, mediating relationships with others – particularly the beneficiaries of social action. Through these processes, pupils can better understand and appreciate important cultural, economic, political, religious, and other similarities and differences.

- *Focused resources and links to curriculum areas*: Community partners can provide resources for planning, implementing, and reflecting on social action, including opening up wider connections to various curriculum areas. The sorts of materials available will, of course, depend on the size and type of the community partner, but most community partners will be happy to work with schools and teachers to co-construct appropriate resources.

Each of these reasons is illustrated in Case Study 6.3.

Case Study 6.3: First Give at The Jo Richardson Community School: Young People as Leaders in the School Community

Isaac Jones, Head of Programmes, First Give, UK

The Jo Richardson Community School has run the First Give (https://firstgive. co.uk/) programme since its inception in 2014. Through the programme, each form group in the year identifies social issues that affect the local community. They choose a charity that is tackling the issue and complete social action in support of their chosen charity. The programme concludes with a celebratory First Give Final in which one group from each form reports on their social action, and advocates for their charity to a panel of judges. The winning form then wins a £1,000 First Give grant for their chosen charity.

In 2019, one form group chose to support the Young Carers of Barking & Dagenham (YCBD). Upon meeting a representative from the organisation, it became clear to them the scale of the issues faced by the charity. They learnt about the number of young people in the borough who acted as young carers and were surprised by the myriad problems that being a young carer could lead to.

One of the young people from the class reflected that: '... *this experience allowed us to open our eyes to the local charities and issues that we hadn't noticed before'.*

They kicked off their social action plan by asking to deliver an assembly to Key Stage 3 (Years 7–9). In this assembly, they explained what a young carer was and reflected on the fact that some young people in the school probably acted as young carers, and their peers might not even realise it. They talked about the support offered by their charity to young carers, and they launched a food collection for YCBD, challenging young people to bring in items that they could donate to the charity.

On top of this, they organised a range of fundraising activities, including raffles, and set themselves the challenge of being able to donate much needed funds to the charity as well as the food bank collection. When the collection of food had been completed, the young people spoke to their teachers and organised for the charity to come to school and collect the donations that had been made throughout the school.

A representative of YCBD said: '*The young people raised enough money to run 3 months' worth of activity, and on top of that collected food and other essential items that supported 65 families who use our foodbank. First Give has been a fantastic way to build our youth supporter network in the community'.*

The double benefit of youth social action means that not only did the programme lead to real and tangible impact for the charity and their clients, but the young people themselves gained enormously. Having been inspired by the 'real-world' nature of the programme, these young people developed empathy; exercised and improved their skills in project planning, public speaking, and teamwork; and became confident leaders within the school community.

Director of Sixth Form at the Jo Richardson Community School, Karen Evans said: '*First Give has allowed our young people to develop teamworking skills, use their creativity to carry out social action and develop an understanding of charities and issues in their area. It has been invaluable to our sixth form'.*

Schools are well known for running fundraising and charity events for young people to participate in, but the real benefit of the First Give programme is the autonomy that young people are given. They research the issues, they choose the charities they want to support, and, as such, they understand the impact they are having. This opportunity to lead on the planning of social action projects is extremely powerful.

Reflective Activity 6.2: Researching community partners

Undertake your own research to identify three community partners relevant to your own region/context. One of these should be a local community partner, one a national/global community partner, and one an intermediary community partner (i.e. an organisation that works to support and facilitate schools' and pupils' social action programmes). For each of these community partners consider the following:

- Looking back at Fig. 6.1, what examples of social action could be developed?
- What educational resources are already provided and what resources could you develop as a teacher?
- How will engaging with this partner support pupils in your school?

A crucial area that we have only touched upon so far in this chapter is the importance of teachers supporting pupils to make connections between their experiences in school and those in wider communities – whether those fostered through schooling or by pupils' associations outside of schools (their families, their neighbourhoods, their faith communities, and so on). A further important area for teachers to consider is the extent to which existing structures and processes within their school support – or indeed inhibit – pupil voice. An open, discursive, and democratic environment *within* the school provides a vital foundation for democratic forms of social action *beyond* the school. Where such practices are part of the very fabric of a school, pupils are valued for the knowledge, experiences, cultures, and interests they bring with them to educational spaces. In other words, if pupils are respected, listened to, and are involved in decision-making processes as a routine part of their experience of schooling, they will be able to take the dispositions learned into their social action activities. Once again, and as we have suggested throughout this book, a positive culture and ethos driven by committed leadership is crucial in creating a school culture that empowers pupils to be creative and critical in developing and expressing their character.

Conclusion

In this chapter, we have introduced youth social action – or service-learning – as a key pedagogical approach for character education, one that when effective and planned intentionally can support both personal and community development. When pupils are engaged in meaningful social action, they understand such action as an educational process underpinned by a moral purpose. Indeed, where the focus of social action is driven by the concerns and desires of pupils themselves, personal and community development will be stronger. When moral purpose, service, and learning combine in collaboration with community partners, pupils are connected to their wider communities through citizenship. This process and practice enables pupils to both cultivate and express a range of moral, intellectual, civic, and performance virtues, from teamwork to leadership, compassion to trust, curiosity to open-mindedness, service to community awareness.

Notes

1   https://www.character.org/11-principles-framework
2   https://www.iwill.org.uk/about-us/youth-social-action
3   https://www.iwill.org.uk/wp-content/uploads/2019/05/iwill-impact-report-1.pdf
4   RSA4 is a youth social action programme for primary aged children. More details can be found at: https://www.rsaacademies.org.uk/projects/rsa4-primary-youth-social-action/

Further reading

Body, A. and Hogg, E. (2019) What mattered ten years on? Young people's reflections on their involvement with a charitable youth participation project, *Journal of Youth Studies*, 22 (2): 171–186.
This article draws on the views and perspectives of ten people who undertook youth participation projects ten years previously. For many of these ten people, their experiences were 'transformative'. Particularly important were the relationships they developed with others and the sense that involvement had helped them in 'finding a voice to affect community decisions'.

Eyler, J. and Giles, D.E. (1999) *Where's the Learning in Service-Learning?* San Francisco, CA: Jossey-Bass.
Though now over 20 years old, a seminal book in the international literature. It focuses on service-learning within universities, but examines a range of intra- and inter-personal qualities developed through the integration of service and learning in community settings.

Seider, S., Kelly, L., Clark, S., Jennett, P., El-Amin, A., Graves, D. et al. (2020) Fostering the socio-political development of African American and Latinx adolescents to analyse and challenge racial and economic inequality, *Youth and Society*, 52 (5): 756–794.
An article that examines the socio-political development of pupils in urban school settings. Utilising a mixed-methods approach, the research studied over 400 pupils attending two different types of high schools: 'progressive' and 'no-excuses'. The study found that pupils in 'progressive' schools showed meaningful development in their abilities to critically analyse racial and economic inequalities, while those in 'no-excuses' schools evidenced meaningful growth in motivation to 'challenge these inequities through activism'.

7 Developing practice and further resources

Introduction

Throughout this book, we have asked you to engage with and examine character education as a planned and intentional approach to pupils' personal and social development. In doing so, we have focused on many core aspects of character education, drawing on real-life case studies to exemplify approaches and strategies. In this final chapter, we introduce some additional practices through which you can develop your own practice further. While we only introduce these to you, we also provide a list of further resources to support you in progressing and extending your understanding of character education.

Chapter Objectives

By the end of this chapter, you should have:

- Considered some further methods and activities that can be used as part of character education
- Familiarised yourself with and researched further resources on character education
- Understood the main principles underpinning different teaching and learning methods in character education.

Developing your teaching and learning methods in character education

Teaching character through stories

Using stories to teach about moral character is not a new approach. One of the reasons that stories are so popular as an educational resource is because of their appeal to teachers and children alike. Stories are engaging resources that are available in abundance and are relevant to the lives of children (Edgington, 2002). The appeal of stories largely lies in their ability to engage the imagination and to entertain. Lickona (1991: 79) explains that stories have always formed part of moral teaching, adding that stories communicate through:

> attraction rather than compulsion; they invite rather than impose. They capture the imagination and touch the heart. All of us have experienced the power

of a good story to stir strong feelings. That's why storytelling is such a natural way to engage and develop the emotional side of a child's character.

Based on this understanding, stories are not just engaging forms of entertainment and amusement; they are a potentially powerful vehicle for character education that can engage children's minds and emotions, and motivate and inspire.

Before discussing how stories can be used to teach about virtues, let us briefly consider why stories are so appealing to schools and teachers from a practical standpoint. In both primary and secondary education, stories permeate the curriculum. Because of the emphasis on reading and literature-related activities within primary schools, there is a great deal of potential for the integration of stories within a school's character education provision (Helterbran, 2009). It is common, for example, for primary schools to use stories as the basis for topic planning – a great story will not just be used for English lessons, but as the context for geography, mathematics, art, and for the learning of other subjects. In secondary schools, longer and more complex stories – in their various forms – naturally feature heavily in English lessons, but also appear in subjects including history, geography, and modern languages.

The use of stories as a vehicle for character education in schools has been advocated by academics and teachers alike. Carr and Harrison (2015: 2) suggest that the 'use of stories from past and present day imaginative literature is perhaps the most promising and potent' route for the education of moral character. Bohlin's (2005) *Teaching Character Education through Literature* and Carr and Harrison's (2015) *Educating Character through Stories* explore the philosophical underpinnings of educating character through stories, and both set out a framework for how children can learn through their engagement with the texts. Of course, stories are not limited to fiction and may come in various genres, lengths, and formats, including short picture books, fables, stories from history, biographies, and recounted events. In addition, stories are told through different forms, including oral retellings, and those told through art, drama, television, and film. There are a number of ways that children can learn about character virtues through stories, and in Box 7.1 we provide an overview of some of the main principles underlying story-based character education.

Research suggests that story-based approaches to character education can increase children's knowledge and understanding of virtue terms, and can develop children's reasoning about moral issues (see, for example, Arthur et al., 2014; Francis et al., 2018; Jónsson et al., 2019). Through engaging with characters' experiences in stories, pupils can be helped to consider and understand 'how to deal with life's conundrums, perplexities, ambitions, motives, attitudes, actions, explanations, feelings, values, ideas, and human types' (Gregory, 2009: 36). It is also thought that engaging with story characters helps to develop virtue emotion, such as through compassionate engagement with characters' 'thoughts, intentions, feelings, behaviour and circumstances' (D'Olimpio and Peterson, 2018: 98). D'Olimpio and Peterson suggest that through this engagement the reader develops a feeling of care towards fictional characters, which

---

Box 7.1: The main principles of character education through stories

Stories can:

- be used throughout the curriculum
- be engaging and entertaining vehicles for character education
- be told through various forms
- enable readers to imaginatively experience new situations and contexts that may not be possible in their own lives
- provide insight into characters' thoughts, feelings, and motivations
- provide a fictional 'safe space' in which pupils can consider alternative courses of action without real-life consequences
- be used to develop virtue perception, virtue knowledge and understanding, virtue reasoning, etc.
- provide models of good (and poor) character
- illustrate the consequences of virtue (and vice)
- convey moral messages or information to the reader.

---

can be applied to others in real-life encounters and eventually becomes engrained, through habituation, in the reader's character.

Furthermore, the vicarious experiences that stories provide enable readers to experience new situations and contexts that may not be possible in their own lives. Through these new experiences, readers have the opportunity to practise or 'rehearse' how they might act if they were in the character's shoes. The unique advantage of stories is that they often provide insight into characters' thoughts, feelings, and motivations – features we do not often get insight into in real life. A skilled teacher can facilitate discussions amongst pupils, helping them to unpick characters' choices, think through potential motivations, as well as suggest alternative courses of action characters may have taken. The role of teachers as facilitators in pupils' learning from stories is even more important when we consider that moral messages conveyed in stories are not always understood as intended, especially by younger pupils (see, for example, Narvaez et al., 1998; Whitney et al., 2005). Thus, teachers play an important role in helping pupils to take appropriate meaning from stories. They can help pupils to relate this meaning to their own lives – and this is something that pupils may find challenging without support, especially when story contexts and character features are unfamiliar.

Using moral dilemmas

Moral dilemmas are stories centred on protagonists who are engaged in difficult situations and who have a number of potentially viable options available to them. Moral philosophers often use moral dilemmas to bring to light and examine overarching moral theories and principles. For the purpose of character education, however, teachers can use moral dilemmas as a way of engaging pupils in reflecting about real-life situations requiring an ethical response. Pupils can discuss, debate, and reflect on dilemmas, and can be encouraged to respond to them, explaining and justifying why they think their chosen response is appropriate. The types of question asked might include:

- What were the challenges faced by the protagonist?
- What virtues are relevant to the dilemma?
- Are different virtues in conflict, and which should be prioritised in the situation and why?
- What would you do if you were the protagonist?
- What would you advise a friend to do if they were the protagonist?

As these questions indicate, the successful use of moral dilemmas can guide and support pupils into asking and answering questions about a variety of virtues, often exploring a clash or conflict between two or more virtues.

Identifying dilemmas which can be used to sustain pupils' interest is an important element of their use in character education. The moral dilemmas used across a school's curriculum should be believable and relevant to pupils, and the stories must have an element of controversy to generate a sufficient range of options, both reasonable and problematic. If all pupils see the dilemma in the same way, there will be very little to explore and discuss. To make effective use of moral dilemmas, teachers can also use them to help evaluate how pupils apply their understanding of character and virtues in a real-life context. Moral dilemmas can fit within and across the curriculum. Debate and discussion of dilemmas fit naturally within most, if not all, subjects; and they can also be explored outside of the formal curriculum, such as in form/home time using local, national, and world news stories to stimulate relevant discussions.

Box 7.2 provides an example of a moral dilemma that could be used with pupils in a lesson. A teacher's approach when using dilemmas will naturally vary depending on the needs of their pupils. Pupils could first be encouraged to identify and discuss the virtues in conflict for each protagonist. Pupils could then share their views on what the protagonists should (or shouldn't) do and how the protagonists' actions may have repercussions – both for them and for others. It is important that teachers encourage pupils to justify their choices; in some dilemmas, there may not be a clear 'right' course of action and through discussion pupils will be able to engage with different perspectives and gain insight into others' moral reasoning. Of course, there is value in varying the structure of the discussion – an alternative approach would be to encourage pupils to share their opinions first, and to then unpick the virtues that are relevant or in conflict. Pupils can then revisit their choices and justifications in light of the discussion.

Box 7.2: An example of a moral dilemma

Priya was never in trouble at home or in school. On Monday morning, Priya was running late for her first lesson and ran into the school corridor to quickly get some books from her locker. Priya's friend, Ethan, was also rushing to get some books and, as he ran through the door, something bad happened. The force Ethan used to close the door caused the glass in the door to shatter. Priya and Ethan panicked and ran to their lessons. That afternoon, there was a whole-school assembly and Priya could tell that Mrs Wilson, the head-teacher, was not happy. Mrs Wilson asked the whole school if they knew anything about the broken door. No one answered. Priya was so scared about getting Ethan into trouble that she remained silent.

The next day, Priya found out that someone from the school office had seen another pupil, Jonathan, hanging around in the corridor just before the glass shattered. Jonathan was regularly in trouble at school and had previously been suspended for breaking a window on purpose. Jonathan had been in to see Mrs Wilson and, despite denying responsibility, Jonathan was given a detention. When discussing the incident with Ethan after school, Ethan said that he would not tell Mrs Wilson the truth and that, if Priya was truly his friend, she would stay quiet. Priya felt relieved that Ethan was not in trouble but deep down felt so guilty that Jonathan was in trouble for something he hadn't done.

That night, Priya couldn't sleep because she kept thinking about Jonathan, Ethan, and the broken door. It just wasn't right.

Reflective Activity 7.1: Using moral dilemmas

How could you use the moral dilemma described in Box 7.2 with pupils? What virtues could be focused upon when doing so? Can you think of other moral dilemmas, relevant to pupils' lives, that can be used to explore other virtue conflicts?

Using moral exemplars

There is growing evidence that suggests pupils can learn by observing adults. The actions and behaviour of adults send out moral messages that have implicit meanings to pupils, even if the adult is not aware of this (Willemse et al., 2008). In Chapter 2, you were introduced to how role-modelling by teachers is an influential strategy in pupils' personal and character development. Role-modelling education in schools occurs primarily through the models set by adults in the school community (this includes all stakeholders). Through a conscious approach to role-modelling, it is hoped that pupils cultivate virtues by observing them in others (Berkowitz and Bier, 2005). However, teachers also regularly use moral exemplars taken from 'real life' or from literature to inspire pupils to emulate character virtues. The effectiveness of using moral exemplars in this way is less clear, and exactly how pupils learn from exemplars has not been extensively explored.

Walker (2016) is an advocate of using moral exemplars to support personal and character development, and he suggests that moral exemplars can fascinate and inspire pupils because their behaviour is largely outside of our own lived experience. In this way, moral exemplars can enthuse pupils to reflect and discuss the character virtues demonstrated. Kristjánsson (2007: 37) advocates for a more direct approach, arguing that 'children must be taught about right and wrong in a more straightforward manner, [and that] moral virtue must seep into them from an early age like dye into wool …, learn[ing] to take their cue from worthy mentors and moral exemplars'.

If we were to survey the general public about who to highlight as moral exemplars, the most popular responses would likely include individuals such as Martin Luther King, Jr, Florence Nightingale, Mahatma Gandhi, Nelson Mandela, and Mother Teresa. We should also recognise that when asked about moral exemplars in their own lives, pupils will often also cite those close to them – in particular members of their families. There are almost endless examples of individuals exemplifying 'good' character, and teaching about them should be encouraged. However, some concerns have been expressed about the 'gap' that can exist between pupils and inspirational people when the life of an inspirational person seems so far removed from pupils' own experiences (Vos, 2018). Through their research based on young people's engagement with voluntary service, Han et al. (2017) suggest that attainable and relevant moral exemplars may be more effective than inspirational exemplars in encouraging young people to engage themselves. To ensure this gap is bridged, teachers must think carefully about the moral exemplars they wish to prioritise and choose a varied selection that crosses the boundaries of inspirational moral exemplars from history and contemporary life to moral exemplars who resonate with the pupil population of the school.

Reflective Activity 7.2: Which role models?

Which individuals – in the school, local community, or more broadly – would you highlight to pupils as being a moral exemplar? What is it about these individuals and their actions that pupils could learn from and be inspired by? How could you structure and scaffold pupils' learning about the moral exemplar to help them learn about and through the lives of the moral exemplar?

Teaching about the lives and actions of moral exemplars can help pupils to critically reflect on their own actions and beliefs. It is important that pupils should not set out to exactly emulate the exemplar, but should look at the character virtues embodied in that individual and the virtuous behaviours they display to explore the meaning and lived enactment of virtues, including when and how they are relevant to their own lives. Case Study 7.1 suggests how teachers might use resources focused on inspirational individuals to teach about character in their lessons.

Case Study 7.1: Amazing People Schools

SELENA WHITEHEAD, Education Team Manager, Amazing People Schools

Intelligence plus character – that is the goal of true education.
— Martin Luther King, Jr.

Harriet Tubman knew all about resilience. Einstein used wildly creative ideas in his scientific work. Character strengths such as empathy, perseverance, and gratitude greatly improve the odds that our young people will thrive, regardless of the challenges.

Amazing People Schools is an award-winning online character education platform that's loved by teachers, embraced by schools, and is changing the lives of pupils. We bring to life the incredible stories of game-changers from history – ordinary people who used their character strengths to help them achieve extraordinary things. Our site is built around an inspirational, interactive story library that was researched by psychologist Dr Charles Margerison over a period of more than two decades, exploring not just what these people did but how and why they did it. Dr Margerison was ahead of the curve in his now well-documented belief that character strengths play a vital role in pupil wellbeing, social emotional learning, and positive personal development. Amazing People Schools supports young people to harness these innate character strengths, believe in themselves, and flourish. We work with schools around the world and were one of the first companies to be accreditated with the Company of Character Kitemark by the Association for Character Education.

How it works
The inspirational stories of our diverse collection of Amazing People are explored through the lens of character through video, audio, timelines, and written stories, and are accessible directly by pupils or as part of a teacher-led programme. The diverse nature of our website is so important – we believe that 'you can't be it if you can't see it'. Our work with schools has highlighted that pupils do look for themselves in these stories and seek out characters who inspire them.

We support the weaving of character into the fabric of schools. When the language of character is truly embedded in the day-to-day, the postive impact really takes effect. Our video content clearly links character strengths with individuals – Da Vinci's creativity, for example, or Frida Kahlo's resilience. Our timelines highlight key dates in the amazing person's life and character strengths that supported them at pivotal moments. Pupils are invited at the end of the story to assess the top three strengths the amazing person displayed. Having explored their character fully, pupils are invited to take a quiz and, on gaining full marks, can customise their avatar with wardrobe items;

perhaps Albert Einstein's shock of wild hair or Frida Kahlo's vibrant flowers. To ensure pupils feel connected to the topic, they are also encouraged to answer the question, 'who do you think is amazing?' This can be anyone that matters to them, from a famous footballer or musican to a family member who has overcome difficulties.

A wide variety of resources created by teachers, for teachers, accompany the storytelling and these help to embed the teaching of character right across the curriculum. For example, there are assemblies which look at a given character strength, such as gratitude, and use the stories of people including Helen Keller and Louis Armstrong to explore this further. The assemblies also provide an opportunity to explain how practising gratitude increases resilience, happiness, and optimism. Reflection is given priority so pupils can learn from Helen Keller's attitude to gratitude: how we can take time to appreciate what we have and who we have in our lives.

Form time is an another ideal way to discuss character and our flexible, ready-to-use lessons are a quick and easy way into this. Each lesson examines a different character strength and uses a specific role model to illustrate that strength in their lives. So, for example, a lesson may cover curiosity using Leonardo da Vinci or Mary Seacole.

Wellbeing and character

The link between character and wellbeing is so important. The provision of inspirational stories, and the tools and language to build character and bolster wellbeing, can prove invaluable and life-changing. Our popular Wellbeing Workouts are extremely important in this way. Character strengths such as kindness, gratitude, optimism, and resilience – when practised regularly – support social emotional learning and wellbeing. Our workouts either focus on a given strength and several exemplars who demonstrate that strength, or an amazing person and several strengths that they demonstrate. For example, Mahatma Gandhi's workout explores creativity, self-discipline, and empathy, with activities to help pupils to 'flex their character muscles' and build mental strength by developing these strenghts within themselves.

Through our work at Amazing People Schools, we seek to provide an instant, flexible programme of stories and resources that can be used in a myriad of ways across a school curriculum. Schools and teachers can bend and flex our programme to fit their needs, school community and values. It is ideal for blended learning and is constantly being updated to bring in new stories and resources.

Amazing People Schools is free to explore: www.amazingpeopleschools.com

Cultivating practical wisdom

The development of practical wisdom is a core concern for character educators who take their inspiration from Aristotle. There remains, however, important questions about how practical wisdom develops and at what age practical wisdom is possible, and there has been surprisingly little written about how practical wisdom might be taught and learned (see Kristjánsson, 2015; Kristjánsson et al., 2020). Central to these questions is the 'paradox' of how children move from habituation to critical reflection and on to practical wisdom. The philosopher Myles Burnyeat (2012) does not envisage practical wisdom education to be possible until after a long period of strict habituation, possibly not until late adolescence or early adulthood. For many in the field of character development, Burnyeat's interpretation leaves the transition between childhood and moral maturity unexplained, and it does seem unreasonable to think that children are not developing some important critical faculties before adolescence. In this vein, the philosopher Nancy Sherman (1989) argues that full virtue develops at an uneven rate and pace and that through experiences of trial, error, and enquiry, practical wisdom will develop. Though young children may lack the more developed deliberative skills of older children, this does not imply the absence of other cognitive capacities relevant to the development of practical wisdom. If, as we would suggest it should be, practical wisdom is understood as challenging and always a work in progress (even in adulthood), it might be better to understand the work of teachers and schools as supporting pupils to learn, experience, and reflect in ways shaped by the goal of practical wisdom (or, as one primary headteacher recently put it in a conversation, 'in the spirit of practical wisdom').

To attempt to develop practical wisdom in young people is not an easy task, though teachers implementing character education accept the challenge and try not to overly 'water down' complicated concepts (Harrison, 2016: 5). These teachers embrace difficult conversations with pupils, using the language of character to navigate this terrain. The spiral curriculum model introduced in Chapter 5 has been drawn on by Hatchimonji et al. (2020) as a potential curriculum model for the teaching and development of practical wisdom. In explaining the strengths of a spiral curriculum, Hatchimonji et al. (2020: 134) remind us that the formation of character does not follow clear and linear stages. Rather:

> virtues and skills are interdependent; the development of generosity potentiates the development of emotion regulation and vice versa. Further, situational context influences the expression of competency such that for individuals with particular sets of knowledge, skill, and motivation, some situations will evoke a higher level of virtue application than others.

While the precise contours of educating practical wisdom in schools remain under-researched, and while the attainment of practical wisdom is 'an aspirational goal' (Hatchimonji et al., 2020: 136), educating children in the spirit of practical wisdom is not an altogether alien task. Schools routinely teach children to think critically, to notice and consider important features of situations they and others encounter, to think about their life goals (and the life goals of others), to make explicit their reasons, emotions, actions, and motivations, and, importantly, to reflect on each in order to learn and grow. It is qualities such as these – intentionally taught and brought together in unison – that can help pupils to not only know what is good, but also act accordingly.

Continuing your professional development

While all teachers influence the character of their pupils, the strength of character education in a school depends a great deal on whether all teachers (and indeed other staff) commit to the process and share the mission and vision of the school. Teachers also need to be supported in this endeavour through having access to high-quality, research-informed, and practically focused continuing professional development. Schools must support teachers by investing time and effort in continuing professional development on and about character education, including allowing them to come together to discuss ideas, share practice, and learn together (Arthur et al., 2015c).

Professional development in character education is best when the focus is consistent and targeted, and is coupled with regular and honest self-evaluation. Case Study 7.2 demonstrates how well-focused professional development can enable all staff to grow and flourish as character educators.

Case Study 7.2: Character Education and Continuing Professional Development in School

LYDIA DUFFY, History Teacher, Selly Park Girls' School, Birmingham, UK

Beginning the journey into character education
When character education was initially introduced in our school, it seemed like a difficult but crucial framework to devise. The aim was to create a school ethos centred on character virtues, where character education would eventually be delivered seamlessly throughout subject curriculums and extra-curricular activities. We began by ascertaining which character virtues were most relevant to our school community. During whole-school continuing professional development (CPD) sessions, teaching staff were asked to reflect on the character virtues that we believed were most important for our pupils to develop, reflecting on our current teaching practices to evaluate if these virtues were present already. After a vigorous process of discussions and ranking we decided on ten virtues (see Case Study 3.2).

CPD to support teaching
In order for character education to be embedded in the ethos and curriculums of the school, members of staff received a variety of CPD sessions. The initial CPD sessions were tailored around developing knowledge and understanding of character education. As part of the sessions, staff also discussed the existing opportunities pupils had to develop character virtues and how these could be linked to the development of the school's new core virtues. These sessions allowed staff to offer their opinions, as well as motivating them to take ownership of the developments that were taking place. This encouraged many members of staff, myself included, to begin to reflect on the impact that their teaching has upon the character of a child, and this in turn motivated us to want to continue to improve what we offered as a school.

During ongoing CPD sessions on the implementation of character education, we have been given time and the resources to be able to explore the academic literature in the field. This has provided evidence on the successful delivery of character education and the potential impact it can have upon pupils. The focus on academic literature has allowed us, as professionals, to expand our knowledge of education practices. Another focus of CPD sessions has been the practical application of new ideas and methods. The Heads of House regularly lead CPD sessions offering ideas on how to implement the teaching of virtues into lessons, supporting teaching staff to weave character into subject curriculums. This also offers teachers an opportunity to celebrate their work promoting character education, and also offers practical 'teaching and learning' ideas. The ability to come together to share ideas is invaluable for all staff, particularly members of staff who, like me, are in the early years of a career in education. Sharing examples of good practice gives teachers the confidence to deliver character education within their lessons and around school.

CPD to develop the character of the teacher

As much as CPD is often focused on teaching and learning techniques, character education CPD also offers a more personal level of development for teachers. When deciding upon the virtues to incorporate into the school's ethos, we were asked to reflect upon what virtues were important to us and upon the root reasoning for education. We focused on how education has the power to shape and form positive members of society. This space for reflection has allowed us to consider the importance of our role as teachers and has inspired us to want to improve the education we offer to pupils. It has also helped us to ensure that, as teachers, we are acting as role models in actively and positively shaping the next generation of citizens.

The impact on my own practice

The education I have received through CPD sessions has provided me with the confidence to discuss my expectations of pupils within lessons, using the language of virtue to encourage positive actions. Engaging in CPD with colleagues has also encouraged me to ensure my lessons cover a broad and balanced curriculum, for example, using the virtue of aspiration to discuss careers and inspire ambitious pupils. I have used the virtues of service and compassion to explore difficult historical topics and encourage pupils to have meaningful discussions about national and global issues. The CPD sessions at school have also enabled me – and indeed all staff – to build connections with the work of other schools. We have, for example, enlisted the support of the Association for Character Education to deliver CPD, providing us with an external perspective and advice on how to deliver character education through teaching, as well as increasing our knowledge of current academic research and practice in other schools.

As indicated in Case Study 7.2 and some of the other case studies throughout this book, schools that have been successful in developing a character education approach have actively sought to use research within the field of character education as a core foundation for their continuing professional development programmes. Some schools use designated time within staff meetings or staff training to facilitate staff to engage with and read research. Other examples of possible professional development sessions include:

- *Whole-school in-service training*: regular extended staff development sessions focused on building and extending a character education approach within a school. For example, weekly activities where staff are supported in the delivery of character education within their classrooms and curriculums, or activities where staff examine their character resources alongside each other or with external experts.
- *Drop-in sessions*: opportunities for staff to receive more directed and personal character education professional development. These could include focus on specific topics, such as developing character through subjects, character through behaviour management and pastoral care; or developing the use of the language of character within the school.
- *Shared activities*: character evaluation presentations from staff across the school showcasing good practice, with opportunities for staff at all levels in the school to come together to discuss, share, and learn.

There are many organisations, research centres, and other educational providers that provide continuing professional development in character education, including by offering postgraduate programmes in character education. Engaging in postgraduate study can help to not only develop the teacher undertaking the course of study, but their professional setting – as Case Study 7.3 illustrates.

Case study 7.3: Developing Character Education Practice through Postgraduate Study

Lois Banks, Assistant Headteacher, Hoo St Werburgh Primary School and Marlborough Centre, Hoo, UK

While teaching and looking to develop character education in a previous school in which I worked, I undertook a master's programme of study at a local university. Part of my master's research explored the formation of young children's perceptions of character in a large three-form entry infant and nursery school in Medway, Kent. At the time of the study, Medway was reported to have 38 per cent of their children underperforming academically in schools. The study investigated how twenty teachers and parents viewed both their own and each other's role in developing good character and then compared these to the children's perceptions. The study also followed three focus pupils, aged 4–5 years. The evidence was gathered through a mosaic approach of observations, interviews, child-led walks, and photography.

Character was not a term many of the practitioners had heard of and therefore our first step was some exploration about character through weekly continuing professional development sessions. Practitioners were given time in groups to research what character meant to them and how it can be developed in school. At first staff were a little hesitant but after some time their confidence and ideas really grew. The Jubilee Centre for Character and Virtues' *A Framework for Character Education in Schools* (2017) was introduced to staff and was compared to frameworks staff had researched themselves. This was the start of the school's character journey, but as teachers started teaching stand-alone character lessons, they recognised that the school was still missing the valuable experiences and insight of our children and their families.

Parent interviews were set up to determine how character was regarded at home and it was clear they all believed the teacher should play a part in developing children's character. However, parents also thought character should be developed in partnership with parents.

Interestingly, and echoing research by Harrison et al. (2018), the teacher interviews highlighted a general opinion that parents preferred a focus on the academic outcomes rather than on character – something not confirmed in the parent interviews. Teachers were, however, very keen to work alongside parents on their journey.

During the child-led interviews, scenarios were given to the children and they were asked what they would do in each situation. The children often referenced their parents, saying things such as: 'My daddy says it's better to tell the truth and it makes you happy', and 'My mummy said don't give up when it's hard'. These insights reminded us how important families are in shaping young children's character, and how this needed to be reflected in our work in school.

Using the building blocks of character and drawing on the experience of parents, teachers, and children, the school devised their own, age-appropriate, STAR framework with physical soft toys to represent each virtue: Sammy Seal (Success), Temi Turtle (Teamwork), Adam Ant (Aspiration), and Rocky Raccoon (Respect). Teachers noticed that the children were exceptionally quick in engaging with the STAR framework, and the vocabulary was soon heard being used throughout the school by adults and children.

The children have guided the further implementation of character into the school and are a part of many decisions made within the school. The children attend a character assembly each week, which was formerly where the teachers handed out a certificate for great writing or other academic focused achievements. Now, the children lead and host the assembly independently, and ask their peers which virtues they have shown or struggled to show that week.

Placing character at the heart of the school has led to some transformational progress. The biggest achievement of all for the school has been the change in the behaviour and conduct of the children. The teachers set up class debates from Nursery to Year 2 to ask pupils how they could improve the behaviour charts used in classrooms and the school. At the time, a name on the peg was either put on a sun (where they all started), a star (for something amazing), or a rain cloud (when they had done something deemed wrong by the teacher). The children all agreed that when they had to walk across the classroom and put their name on the cloud it made them feel bad, and the teachers agreed it felt like they were demeaning the child rather than supporting them to make good choices. The children devised a new system where all of the pegs started on the star and the teachers moved the peg on to either Sammy Seal, Temi Turtle, Adam Ant, or Rocky Raccoon when a child demonstrated that particular virtue. This developed further into the teacher telling pupils, 'I've just seen you using a STAR virtue', and the child putting their peg on the virtue they thought they had demonstrated, explaining why. The use of sanctions reduced, and the behaviour across school dramatically improved in a very short period.

We now turn our attention to further resources that you can access and engage with.

Further resources

Below we set out links to, and descriptions of, some well-known organisations that conduct research, support teachers, and provide resources for character education. We recommend that you visit the websites linked below and explore the resources available to you. These will be relevant whether you are a beginning teacher or a teacher seeking to access quality continuing professional development resources. We hope that, in addition to our guidance and the case studies we have collated, you will be able to take inspiration from these sources, using them to develop your own knowledge and understanding of character education.

Association for Character Education
https://character-education.org.uk/
The Association for Character Education (ACE) is based in the UK and is a 'community for schools, organisations and individuals interested in character education to share expertise and practice'.[1] ACE aims to support schools and teachers in the development and enhancement of their character education provision. ACE runs an annual conference and provides professional development training for schools. ACE also evaluates character education provision in schools and other education organisations, awarding a kitemark, which provides recognition for character education. ACE's 'School of Character Kitemark' or 'Kitemark Plus' is awarded to schools and colleges that can demonstrate that they take an explicit, planned, and reflective approach to the cultivation of character. Members of ACE can access character education resources, including blogs and guides written for teachers.

Center for Character and Citizenship
www.characterandcitizenship.org
The University of Missouri-St Louis' Center for Character and Citizenship is a research centre focused on the development of character, democratic citizenship,

and civil society. The Center for Character and Citizenship engages in research and seeks to generate and share knowledge about how character develops. The Center provides teachers with resources and toolkits to support their practice, including offering a range of professional development courses and resources for researchers, educators, and parents.

Character.org
www.character.org
Character.org is a US-based educational organisation 'devoted to fostering character development in our schools and communities'[2] whose *11 Principles Framework*[3] was introduced in Chapter 1. The framework sets out a guide to cultivating a culture of character in a school and Character.org evaluates schools on their implementation of the principles, certifying successful schools as 'National Schools of Character'. On their website, Character.org sets out what they believe makes a school of character and provides teachers with examples of schools' 'promising practices' – school-based character initiatives that are examples of effective character education.

Character Lab
www.characterlab.org
Character Lab is an organisation that connects researchers and teachers and seeks to create greater knowledge about what contributes to social, emotional, academic, and physical wellbeing for young people in the US. Character Lab provide 'Tips' and 'Playbooks' to support teachers. The 'Tips' are short pieces of advice for teachers implementing character education in schools, whereas 'Playbooks' provide teachers with 'research-based guides to cultivate strengths of heart, mind, and will'.[4]

International Positive Education Network (IPEN)
www.ipen-network.com
In Chapter 1, we introduced you to the work of IPEN and discussed its overlap with positive psychology. IPEN has a vision for education which focuses on character, wellbeing, and resilience in addition to academic study. Through their work, IPEN seeks to *reform policy* – encouraging policymakers to educate for character and wellbeing *alongside* academic study; *change education practice* – equipping teachers with the knowledge and tools to target character and wellbeing, and academic study; and *support collaboration* – developing a community of teachers who can collaborate and learn from one another. In pursuit of these aims, IPEN's website provides teachers with articles and free resources.

Jubilee Centre for Character and Virtues
www.jubileecentre.ac.uk
The Jubilee Centre for Character and Virtues is a research centre based at the University of Birmingham in the UK. The Jubilee Centre's research focuses on the development of character and virtues in individuals and in society – for

example, in schools, at home, in the professions, and within education more broadly. Through its work, the Jubilee Centre seeks to renew a focus on character and virtues in society and is a leading informant on character education policy and practice.

The Jubilee Centre provides resources for teachers that are informed by research and are developed in consultation with experts in the field. On their *Teacher Resources* page,[5] you will find resources that can be used and adapted, including:

- bespoke programmes of study for primary and secondary schools
- subject-based lessons
- story- and poetry-based resources
- character-based assemblies (see the Character Curriculum: KS1–KS4).

The Jubilee Centre also provides free (online) professional development training[6] for aspiring leaders of character education in schools.

Notes

1 https://character-education.org.uk/#about
2 www.character.org/history
3 www.character.org/11-principles-framework
4 www.characterlab.org/playbooks/
5 https://www.jubileecentre.ac.uk/2955/character-education/teacher-resources
6 www.jubileecentre.ac.uk/cpd

References

Arthur, J. (2003) *Education with Character: The Moral Economy of Schooling*. London: RoutledgeFalmer.

Arthur, J. (2014) Traditional approaches to character education in Britain and America, in L. Nucci, D. Narvaez and T. Krettenauer (eds.) *Handbook of Moral and Character Education*, 2nd edition. New York: Routledge.

Arthur, J. (2020) *The Formation of Character in Education: From Aristotle to the 21st Century*. Abingdon: Routledge.

Arthur, J., Davison, J. and Lewis, M. (2005) *Professional Values and Practice: Achieving the Standards for QTS*. Abingdon: Routledge.

Arthur, J., Harrison, T., Carr, D., Kristjánsson, K. and Davison, I. (2014) *Knightly Virtues: Enhancing Virtue Literacy through Stories: Research Report*. Birmingham: University of Birmingham, Jubilee Centre for Character and Virtues. [Online.] Available at: www.jubileecentre.ac.uk/userfiles/jubileecentre/pdf/KVPDF/KnightlyVirtuesReport.pdf

Arthur, J., Harrison, T. and Taylor, E. (2015a) *Building Character through Youth Social Action*. Birmingham: University of Birmingham, Jubilee Centre for Character and Virtues. [Online.] Available at: https://www.jubileecentre.ac.uk/userfiles/jubileecentre/pdf/Research%20Reports/Building_Character_Through_Youth_Social_Action.pdf

Arthur, J., Kristjánsson, K., Cooke, S., Brown, E. and Carr, D. (2015b) *The Good Teacher: Understanding Virtues in Practice: Research Report*. Birmingham: University of Birmingham, Jubilee Centre for Character and Virtues. [Online.] Available at: https://www.jubileecentre.ac.uk/userfiles/jubileecentre/pdf/Research%20Reports/The_Good_Teacher_Understanding_Virtues_in_Practice.pdf

Arthur, J., Kristjánsson, K., Walker, D., Sanderse, W. and Jones, C. (2015c) *Character Education in UK Schools: Research Report*. Birmingham: University of Birmingham, Jubilee Centre for Character and Virtues. [Online.] Available at: https://www.jubileecentre.ac.uk/userfiles/jubileecentre/pdf/Research%20Reports/Character_Education_in_UK_Schools.pdf

Arthur, J., Harrison, T., Burn, E. and Moller, F. (2017a) *Schools of Virtue: Character Education in Three Birmingham Schools: Research Report*. Birmingham: University of Birmingham, Jubilee Centre for Character and Virtues. [Online.] Available at: http://www.jubileecentre.ac.uk/userfiles/jubileecentre/pdf/Research%20Reports/SchoolsOfVirtueResearchReport.pdf

Arthur. J., Harrison, T., Taylor-Collins, E. and Moller, F. (2017b) *A Habit of Service: The Factors that Sustain Service in Young People*. Birmingham: University of Birmingham, Jubilee Centre for Character and Virtues. [Online.] Available at: https://www.jubileecentre.ac.uk/userfiles/jubileecentre/pdf/Research%20Reports/A_Habit_of_Service.pdf

Arthur, J., Kristjansson, K., Harrison, T., Sanderse, W. and Wright, D. (2017c) *Teaching Character and Virtue in Schools*. London: Routledge.

Arthur, J., Fullard, M., Watts, P. and Moller, F. (2018) *Character Perspectives of Student Teachers: Initial Insights*. Birmingham: University of Birmingham, Jubilee Centre for Character and Virtues. [Online.] Available at: https://www.jubileecentre.ac.uk/userfiles/jubileecentre/pdf/projects/TransformativeBritain/Character_Perspectives_Student_Teachers.pdf

Australian Institute for Teaching and School Leadership (2018) *Australian Professional Standards for Teachers, Revised 2018*. Available at: https://www.aitsl.edu.au/teach/standards (accessed 3 February 2021).

Baehr, J. (2017) The varieties of character and some implications for character education, *Journal of Youth Adolescence*, 46 (6): 1153–1161.

Bandura, A. (1977) *Social Learning Theory*. London: Prentice Hall.

Beauchamp, G., Clarke, L., Hulme, M. and Murray, J. (2015) Teacher education in the United Kingdom post devolution: Convergences and divergences, *Oxford Review of Education*, 41 (2): 154–170.

Bennett, T. (2017) *Creating a Culture: How School Leaders can Optimise Behaviour. Independent Review of Behaviour in Schools*. [Online.] Available at: www.gov.uk/government/uploads/system/uploads/attachment_data/file/602487/Tom_Bennett_Independent_Review_of_Behaviour_in_Schools.pdf

Berkowitz, M.W. (2011a) What works in values education, *International Journal of Educational Research*, 50 (3): 153–158.

Berkowitz, M.W. (2011b) Leading schools of character, in A.M. Blankstein and P.D. Houston (eds.) *Leadership for Social Justice and Democracy in Our Schools*. Thousand Oaks, CA: Corwin Press.

Berkowitz, M.W. (2016) *Navigating the semantic minefield of promoting moral development*. Available at: https://www.amenetwork.org/oped/2016/2/15/navigating-the-semantic-minefield-of-promoting-moral-development-by-marvin-w-berkowitz (accessed 3 February 2021).

Berkowitz, M.W. (2021) *PRIMED for Character Education: Six Design Principles for School Improvement*. New York: Routledge.

Berkowitz, M. and Bier, M. (2005) *What Works in Character Education: A Research-Driven Guide for Educators*. Washington, DC: Character Education Partnership.

Berkowitz, M.W. and Hoppe, M.A. (2009) Character education and gifted children, *High Ability Studies*, 20 (2): 131–142.

Berkowitz, M.W., Althof, W. and Bier, M.C. (2012) The practice of pro-social education, in P. Brown, M. Corrigan and A. Higgins-D'Alessandro (eds.) *The Handbook of Prosocial Education* (Vol. 1). Lanham, MD: Rowman & Littlefield.

Berkowitz, M.W., Bier, M. and McCauley, B. (2017) Toward a science of character education: Frameworks for identifying and implementing effective practices, *Journal of Character Education*, 13 (1): 33–51.

Bernacki, M. and Bernt, F. (2007) Service-learning as a transformative experience: An analysis of the impact of service-learning on student attitudes and behaviour after two years of college, in S. Gelmon and S. Billig (eds.) *Service-Learning: From Passion to Objectivity*. Charlotte, NC: Information Age Publishing.

Biesta, G. (2015) What is education for? On good education, teacher judgement, and educational professionalism, *European Journal of Education*, 50: 75–87.

Birdwell, J., Birnie, R. and Mehan, R. (2013) *The State of the Service Nation: Youth Social Action in the UK*. London: Demos. [Online.] Available at: https://www.demos.co.uk/files/Youth_Social_Action_in_the_UK_-_ver_3.pdf?1373620410

Birdwell, J., Scott, R. and Reynolds, L. (2015) *Character Nation: A Demos Report with the Jubilee Centre for Character and Virtues*. London: Demos. [Online.] Available at: http://www.demos.co.uk/files/476_1505_characternation_web.pdf?1433340847

Body, A. and Hogg, E. (2019) What mattered ten years on? Young people's reflections on their involvement with a charitable youth participation project, *Journal of Youth Studies*, 22 (2): 171–186.

Body, A., Lau, E. and Josephidou, J. (2020) The importance of teaching philanthropy: Educating children for the social good, *Impact: Journal of the Chartered College of*

Teaching. [Online.] Available at: https://impact.chartered.college/article/the-importance-of-teaching-philanthropy-educating-children-social-good/ (accessed 3 February 2021).

Bohlin, K. (2005) *Teaching Character Education through Literature.* London: Routledge/ Falmer.

Book, C. and Freeman, D. (1986) Differences in entry characteristics of elementary and secondary teacher candidates, *Journal of Teacher Education,* 37 (2): 47–51.

Bowers, E.P., Johnson, S.K., Buckingham, M.H., Gasca, S., Warren, D.J.A., Lerner, J.V. et al. (2014) Important non-parental adults and positive youth development across mid- to late-adolescence: The moderating effect of parenting profiles, *Journal of Youth and Adolescence,* 43 (6): 897–918.

Brookhart, S. and Freeman, D. (1992) Characteristics of entering teacher candidates, *Review of Educational Research,* 62 (1): 37–60.

Brooks, D. (2016) *The Road to Character.* London: Penguin.

Bruner, J.S. (1960) *The Process of Education.* Cambridge, MA: Harvard University Press.

Bullough, R.V. (2011) Ethical and moral matters in teaching and teacher education, *Teaching and Teacher Education,* 27 (1): 21–28.

Burnyeat, M. (2012) *Explorations in Ancient and Modern Philosophy* (Vol. 2). Cambridge: Cambridge University Press.

Campbell, E. (2008a) Review of the literature: The ethics of teaching as a moral profession, *Curriculum Enquiry,* 38 (4): 357–385.

Campbell, E. (2008b) Teaching ethically as a moral condition of professionalism, in L.P. Nucci and D. Narvaez (eds.) *Handbook of Moral and Character Education.* New York: Routledge.

Carr, D. (2007) Character in teaching, *British Journal of Educational Studies,* 55 (4): 369–389.

Carr, D. and Harrison, T. (2015) *Educating Character through Stories.* Exeter: Imprint Academic.

Character.org (2018) *The 11 Principles of Character. A Validation Framework: for Inspiration, Validation and Certification, Introductory Guide, 2018–2020 Revision.* Available at: https://www.character.org/11-principles-framework (accessed 3 February 2021).

Collaborative for Academic, Social and Emotional Learning (2020) *CASEL's SEL Framework: What Are the Competence Areas and Where Are They Promoted?* [Online.] Available at: https://casel.org/wp-content/uploads/2020/12/CASEL-SEL-Framework-11.2020.pdf

Cooke, S. (2017) The moral work of teaching: A virtue-ethics approach to teacher education, in J. Clandinin and J. Husu (eds.) *The SAGE Handbook of Research on Teacher Education.* London: Sage.

Cooke, S. and Carr, D. (2014) Virtue, practical wisdom and character in teaching, *British Journal of Educational Studies,* 62 (2): 91–110.

Curren, R. and Kotzee, B. (2014) Can virtue be measured?, *Theory and Research in Education,* 12 (3): 266–282.

Davies, I., Evans, M., Fulpp, M., Kiwan, D., Peterson, A. and Sim, J. (2019) *Taking Action for Change: Youth Civic Engagement and Activism. A Resource for Educators.* York: University of York.

Department for Education (DfE) (2013) *Teachers' Standards: Guidance for School Leaders, School Staff and Governing Bodies.* [Online.] Available at: https://assets.publishing.service.gov.uk/government/uploads/system/uploads/attachment_data/file/665520/Teachers__Standards.pdf

Department for Education (DfE) (2016) *Behaviour and Discipline in Schools: Advice for Headteachers and School Staff, January 2016.* [Online.] Available at: https://assets.publishing.service.gov.uk/government/uploads/system/uploads/attachment_ data/file/488034/Behaviour_and_Discipline_in_Schools_-_A_guide_for_headteachers_and_School_Staff.pdf

Department for Education (DfE) (2019a) *Character Education: Framework Guidance, November 2019.* [Online.] Available at: https://assets.publishing.service.gov.uk/government/uploads/system/uploads/attachment_data/file/904333/Character_Education_Framework_Guidance.pdf

Department for Education (DfE) (2019b) *Initial Teacher Training (ITT): Core Content Framework.* [Online.] Available at: https://assets.publishing.service.gov.uk/government/uploads/system/uploads/attachment_data/file/919166/ITT_core_content_ framework_.pdf

Dewey, J. (1933) *How We Think.* London: D.C. Heath.

Diggs, C.R. and Akos, P. (2016) The promise of character education in middle school: A meta-analysis, *Middle Grades Review*, 2 (2): 1–19.

D'Olimpio, L. and Peterson, A. (2018) The ethics of narrative art: Philosophy in schools, compassion and learning from stories, *Journal of Philosophy in Schools*, 5 (1): 92–110.

Duckworth, A. (2016) *Grit: The Power of Passion and Perseverance.* New York: Scribner.

Durlak, J.A., Weissberg, R.P., Dymnicki, A.B., Taylor, R.D. and Schellinger, K.B. (2011) The impact of enhancing students' social and emotional learning: A meta-analysis of school-based universal interventions, *Child Development*, 82 (1): 405–432.

Dweck, C. (2017) *Mindset: Changing the Way You Think to Fulfil Your Potential.* New York: Robinson.

Edgington, W.D. (2002) To promote character education, use literature for children and adolescents, *The Social Studies*, 93 (3): 113–116.

Education Endowment Foundation (EEF) (2019) *Improving Social and Emotional Learning: Guidance Report.* London: EEF. [Online.] Available at: https://educationendowmentfoundation.org.uk/public/files/Publications/SEL/EEF_Social_and_Emotional_Learning.pdf

Education Workforce Council (EWC) (2019) *Codes of Professional Conduct and Practice: For Registrants with the Education Workforce Council (EWC).* Available at: https://www.ewc.wales/site/index.php/en/documents/fitness-to-practice/1754-j16540-ewc-code-of-professional-conduct-e-web.html (accessed 3 February 2021).

Ellis, S. and Tod, J. (2018) *Behaviour for Learning: Promoting Positive Relationships in the Classroom*, 2nd edition. London: Routledge.

Eyler, J. and Giles, D.E. (1999) *Where's the Learning in Service-Learning?* San Francisco, CA: Jossey-Bass.

Fenstermacher, G.D., Osguthorpe, R.D. and Sanger, M.N. (2009) Teaching morally and teaching morality, *Teacher Education Quarterly*, 36 (3): 7–19.

Francis, L.J., Pike, M.A., Lickona, T., Lankshear, D.W. and Nesfield, V. (2018) Evaluating the pilot Narnian Virtues Character Education English Curriculum Project: A study among 11- to 13-year-old students, *Journal of Beliefs and Values*, 39 (2): 233–249.

Fullard, M. (2018) Should we still 'marvel' at comic book heroes?, *Birmingham Blogs: Social Sciences Birmingham.* Available at: https://blog.bham.ac.uk/socialsciencesbirmingham/2018/07/20/comic-con/ (accessed 3 February 2021).

Fullard, M. and Watts, P.M. (2019) Practical wisdom in teaching through the promotion of critical reflection during ITE, in M.A. Peters (ed.) *Encyclopedia of Teacher Education.* Singapore: Springer.

General Teaching Council for Scotland (GTCS) (2021) *The Standard for Full Registration: Mandatory Requirements for Registration with the General Teaching Council for Scotland*, Formal Enactment August 2021. Available at: https://www.gtcs.org.uk/

professional-standards/professional-standards-2021-engagement.aspx (accessed 3 February 2021).

Goleman, D. (1995) *Emotional Intelligence*. New York: Bantam Books.

Gregory, M. (2009) *Shaped by Stories: The Ethical Power of Narratives*. Notre Dame: University of Notre Dame Press.

Han, H., Jeongmin, K., Changwoo, J. and Cohen, G.L. (2017) Attainable and relevant moral exemplars are more effective than extraordinary exemplars in promoting voluntary service engagement, *Frontiers in Psychology*, 8: 283. Available at: https://doi.org/10.3389/fpsyg.2017.00283

Hansen, D.T. (2001) Reflections on the Manner in Teaching Project, *Journal of Curriculum Studies*, 33 (6): 729–735.

Hanson, T., Dietsch, B. and Zheng, H. (2012) *Lessons in Character Impact Evaluation: Final Report* (NCEE 2012-4004). Washington, DC: National Center for Education Evaluation and Regional Assistance, Institute of Education Sciences, US Department of Education. Available at: https://files.eric.ed.gov/fulltext/ED530370.pdf

Harrison, T. (2016) Educating character: From virtue ethics theory to practice, in *Cultivating Virtues: Interdisciplinary Approaches*, Oriel College, Oxford, 7–9 January. Available at: http://jubileecentre.ac.uk/userfiles/jubileecentre/pdf/conference-papers/Cultivating_Virtues/Harrison%2C%20Tom.pdf

Harrison, T., Arthur, J. and Burn, E. (2016a) *Character Education Evaluation Handbook for Schools*. Birmingham: University of Birmingham, Jubilee Centre for Character and Virtues. [Online.] Available at: http://jubileecentre.ac.uk/1721/character-education

Harrison, T., Bawden, M. and Rogerson, L. (2016b) *Teaching Character through Subjects: Educating the Virtues through and within 14 Secondary Subjects*. Birmingham: University of Birmingham, Jubilee Centre for Character and Virtues. [Online.] Available at: http://www.jubileecentre.ac.uk/1676/character-education/resources/teaching-characterthrough-subjects

Harrison, T., Morris, I. and Ryan, J. (2016c) *Teaching Character in the Primary Classroom*. London: Sage.

Harrison, T., Dineen, K. and Moller, F. (2018) *Parent–Teacher Partnerships: Barriers and Enablers to Collaborative Character Education, Initial Insights*. Birmingham: University of Birmingham, Jubilee Centre for Character and Virtues. [Online.] Available at: http://jubileecentre.ac.uk/userfiles/jubileecentre/pdf/projects/TransformativeBritain/ParentTeacher_Partnerships.pdf

Hart, R. (1992) *Children's Participation: From Tokenism to Citizenship*. Florence: UNICEF.

Hart, S. (2007) Service-learning and literacy motivation: Setting a research agenda, in S. Gelmon and S. Billig (eds.) *Service-Learning: From Passion to Objectivity*. Charlotte, NC: Information Age Publishing.

Hatchimonji, D.R., Linsky, A.C.V., Nayman, S.J. and Elias, M.J. (2020) Spiral model of phronesis development: Social-emotional and character development in low-resourced urban schools, *Journal of Moral Education*, 49 (1): 129–142.

Hattie, J. (2009) *Visible Learning: A Synthesis of Over 800 Meta-Analyses Relating to Achievement*. Abingdon: Routledge.

Hecht, D. (2003) The missing link: Exploring the context of learning in service-learning, in S. Billig and J. Eyler (eds.) *Deconstructing Service-Learning: Research Exploring Context, Participation, and Impacts*. Charlotte, NC: Information Age Publishing.

Helterbran, V.R. (2009) Linking character education and global understanding through children's picture books, *Kappa Delta Pi Record*, 45 (2): 69–73.

Hogg, E. (2016) Constant, serial and trigger volunteers: Volunteering across the life course and into older age, *Voluntary Sector Review*, 7 (2): 169–190.

Hopkins, B. (2002) Restorative justice in schools, *Support for Learning*, 13 (3): 144–149.

Hopkins, B. (2004) *Just Schools: A Whole School Approach to Restorative Justice*. London: Jessica Kingsley.

Howard, R.W., Berkowitz, M.W. and Schaeffer, E.F. (2004) Politics of character education, *Educational Policy*, 18 (1): 188–215.

Hursthouse, R. (1999) *On Virtue Ethics*. Oxford: Oxford University Press.

Jeynes, W.H. (2017) A meta-analysis on the relationship between character education and student achievement and behavioral outcomes, *Education and Urban Society*, 49 (1): 1–39.

Johnson, S.K., Buckingham, M.H., Morris, S.L., Suzuki, S., Weiner, M.B., Hershberg, R.M. et al. (2016) Adolescents' character role models: Exploring who young people look up to as examples of how to be a good person, *Research in Human Development*, 13 (2): 126–141.

Jónsson, O.P., Harðarson, A., Sigurðardóttir, Þ.B., Jack, R. and Jóelsdóttir, S.S. (2019) Young people, old literature and character education in Icelandic schools, *Scandinavian Journal of Educational Research*, 1–14. Available at: https://notendur.hi.is/atlivh/textar/skolamal/Young_People_Old_Literature_and_Character_Education_in_Icelandic_Schools.pdf

Joseph, P.B. (2016) Ethical reflections on becoming teachers, *Journal of Moral Education*, 45 (1): 31–45.

Jubilee Centre for Character and Virtues (2014) *Statement on Youth Social Action and Character Development*. Birmingham, University of Birmingham. [Online.] Available at: https://www.jubileecentre.ac.uk/userfiles/jubileecentre/pdf/StatementSocialAction.pdf

Jubilee Centre for Character and Virtues (2017) *A Framework for Character Education in Schools*. Birmingham: University of Birmingham. [Online.] Available at: https://www.jubileecentre.ac.uk/userfiles/jubileecentre/pdf/character-education/Framework%20for%20Character%20Education.pdf

Kohlberg, L. (1987) *The Measurement of Moral Judgement*. Cambridge: Cambridge University Press.

Korthagen, F.A.J. (2004) In search of the essence of a good teacher: Towards a more holistic approach in teacher education, *Teaching and Teacher Education*, 20 (1): 77–97.

Kristjánsson, K. (2006a) 'Emotional intelligence' in the classroom? An Aristotelian critique, *Educational Theory*, 56 (1): 39–56.

Kristjánsson, K. (2006b) Emulation and the use of role models in moral education, *Journal of Moral Education*, 35 (1): 37–49.

Kristjánsson, K. (2007) *Aristotle, Emotions, and Education*. Farnham: Ashgate.

Kristjánsson, K. (2013) Ten myths about character, virtue and virtue education – plus three well-founded misgivings, *British Journal of Educational Studies*, 61 (3): 269–287.

Kristjánsson, K. (2015) *Aristotelian Character Education*. Abingdon: Routledge.

Kristjánsson, K. (2017) Moral education today: Ascendancy and fragmentation, *Journal of Moral Education*, 46 (4): 339–346.

Kristjánsson, K. (2020) *Flourishing as the Aim of Education: A Neo-Aristotelian View*. Abingdon: Routledge.

Kristjánsson, K., Darnell, C., Fowers, B., Moller, F., Pollard, D. and Thoma, S. (2020) *Phronesis: Developing a Conception and an Instrument: Research Report*. Birmingham: University of Birmingham, Jubilee Centre for Character and Virtues. [Online.] Available at: https://www.jubileecentre.ac.uk//userfiles/jubileecentre/pdf/Research%20Reports/Phronesis_Report.pdf

Lamb, M., Taylor-Collins, E. and Silvergate, C. (2019) Character education for social action: A conceptual analysis of the #iwill campaign, *Journal of Social Science Education*, 18 (1): 125–152.

Lapsley, D. and Woodbury, R. (2016) Moral-character development for teacher education, *Action in Teacher Education*, 38 (3): 194–206.

Lickona, T. (1991) *Educating for Character*. New York: Bantam.

Lickona, T. (1996) Eleven principles of effective character education, *Journal of Moral Education*, 25 (1): 93–100.

Lickona, T. (2018) *How to Raise Kind Kids: And Get Respect, Gratitude, and a Happier Family in the Bargain*. New York: Penguin Books.

Lifelong Learning UK (LLUK) (2009) *Northern Ireland Professional Standards for Teachers, Tutors and Trainers in the Lifelong Learning Sector*. [Online.] Available at: http://dera.ioe.ac.uk/190/1/Professional_Standards_for_TTTS_in_NI_-_FINAL_April2009.pdf

Lucas, B. (2019) Character education in schools: An initial overview of some frameworks and associated implementation issues, *Eton Journal for Innovation and Research in Education*, November: 4–9.

Lumpkin, A. (2008) Teachers as role models teaching character and moral virtues, *Journal of Physical Education, Recreation and Dance*, 79 (2): 45–50.

Marshall, L., Rooney, K., Dunatchik, A. and Smith, N. (2017) *Developing Character Skills in Schools: Quantitative Survey*. London: Department for Education. [Online.] Available at: https://dera.ioe.ac.uk/29742/1/Developing_Character_skills-survey_report.pdf

McGrath, H. and Noble, T. (2010) Supporting positive pupil relationships: Research to practice, *Educational and Child Psychology*, 27 (1): 79–90.

McGrath, R. (2018) What is character education? Development of a prototype, *Journal of Character Education*, 14 (2): 23–35.

McLaughlin, C. and Clarke, B. (2010) Relational matters: A review of the impact of school experience on mental health in early adolescence, *Educational and Child Psychology*, 27 (1): 91–103.

Narvaez, D., Bentley, J., Gleason, T. and Samuels, J. (1998) Moral theme comprehension in third graders, fifth graders, and college students, *Reading Psychology: An International Quarterly*, 19 (2): 217–241.

Norrish, J. (2015) *Positive Education: The Geelong Grammar School Journey*. Oxford: Oxford University Press.

Osguthorpe, R.D. (2008) On the reasons we want teachers of good disposition and moral character, *Journal of Teacher Education*, 59 (4): 288–299.

Osguthorpe, R.D. (2013) Attending to ethical and moral dispositions in teacher education, *Issues in Teacher Education*, 22 (1): 17–28.

Peterson, A. and Arthur, J. (2021) *Ethics and the Good Teacher: Character in the Professional Domain*. London: Routledge.

Peterson, C. and Seligman, M.E.P. (2004) *Character Strengths and Virtues: A Handbook and Classification*. Oxford: Oxford University Press.

Revell, L. and Arthur, J. (2007) Character education in schools and the education of teachers, *Journal of Moral Education*, 36 (1): 79–92.

Richardson, V. and Fallona, C. (2001) Classroom management as method and manner, *Journal of Curriculum Studies*, 33 (6): 705–728.

Ruch, W., Platt, T. and Hofmann, J. (2014) The character strengths of class clowns, *Frontiers in Psychology*, 5: 1075. Available at: https://doi.org/10.3389/fpsyg.2014.01075

Ryan, K. and Bohlin, K.E. (1999) *Building Character in Schools: Practical Ways to Bring Moral Instruction to Life*. San Francisco, CA: Jossey-Bass.

Sabol, T.J. and Pianta, R.C. (2012) Recent trends in research on teacher–child relationships, *Attachment and Human Development*, 14 (3): 213–231.

Sanderse, W. (2013) The meaning of role modelling in moral and character education, *Journal of Moral Education*, 42 (1): 28–42.

Sanderse, W. (2015) An Aristotelian model of moral development, *Journal of Philosophy of Education*, 49 (3): 382–398.

Sanger, M.N. (2012) The schizophrenia of contemporary education and the moral work of teaching, *Curriculum Inquiry*, 42 (2): 285–307.

Sanger, M.N. and Osguthorpe, R.D. (2011) Teacher education, preservice teacher beliefs, and the moral work of teaching, *Teaching and Teacher Education*, 27 (3): 569–578.

Sanger, M.N. and Osguthorpe, R.D. (2013) Modeling as moral education: Documenting, analysing, and addressing a central belief of preservice teachers, *Teaching and Teacher Education*, 29 (1): 167–176.

Seider, S., Kelly, L., Clark, S., Jennett, P., El-Amin, A., Graves, D. et al. (2020) Fostering the socio-political development of African American and Latinx adolescents to analyse and challenge racial and economic inequality, *Youth and Society*, 52 (5): 756–794.

Seligman, M.E.P. (2011) *Flourish: A Visionary New Understanding of Happiness and Well-being*. New York: Free Press.

Seligman, M.E.P. and Csikszentmihalyi, M. (2000) Positive psychology: An introduction, *American Psychologist*, 55 (1): 5–14.

Sherman, N. (1989) *The Fabric of Character: Aristotle's Theory of Virtue*. Oxford: Clarendon Press.

Shields, D. (2011) Character as the aim of education, *Phi Delta Kappan*, 92 (8): 48–53.

Smith, G. (2015) *Character Education: A Taught Course for 4 to 11 Year Olds*. Birmingham: University of Birmingham, Jubilee Centre for Character and Virtues. [Online.] Available at: www.jubileecentre.ac.uk/primaryprogramme

Snyder, F.J. (2014) Socio-emotional and character development: A theoretical orientation, *Journal of Character Education*, 10 (2): 107–127.

Steer, A. (2009) *Learning Behaviour. Lessons Learned: A review of behaviour standards and practices in our schools*. Available at: https://webarchive.nationalarchives.gov.uk/20130102204748/https://www.education.gov.uk/publications/standard/publicationDetail/Page1/DCSF-00453-2009 (accessed 3 February 2021).

Taylor-Collins, E., Harrison, T., Thoma, S.J. and Moller, F. (2019) A habit of social action: Understanding the factors associated with adolescents who have made a habit of helping others, *Voluntas: International Journal of Voluntary and Nonprofit Organizations*, 30: 98–114.

The Campaign for Youth Social Action (2013) *Scoping a Quality Framework for Youth Social Action: Summary Slides*. London: The Young Foundation. [Online.] Available at: https://youngfoundation.org/wp-content/uploads/2013/08/Scoping-a-Quality-Framework-for-Youth-Social-Action-FINAL.pdf

Thompson, A. and Metcalfe, J. (2020) Charting the character strengths of #iwill ambassadors, *Impact: Journal of the Chartered College of Teaching*. [Online.] Available at: https://impact.chartered.college/article/charting-the-character-strengths-iwill-ambassadors/ (accessed 3 February 2021).

Tickle, L. (2001) Professional qualities and teacher induction, *Journal of In-Service Education*, 27 (1): 51–64.

Tough, P. (2012) *How Children Succeed: Confidence, Curiosity and the Hidden Power of Character*. New York: Houghton Mifflin Harcourt.

Urban, J.B. and Trochim, W.M. (2017) Advancing evaluation of character building programs, *Journal of Character Education*, 13 (2): 13–27.

Vos, P.H. (2018) Learning from exemplars: Emulation, character formation and the complexities of ordinary life, *Journal of Beliefs and Values*, 39 (1): 17–28.

Wagner, L. and Ruch, W. (2015) Good character at school: Positive classroom behavior mediates the link between character strengths and school achievement, *Frontiers in Psychology*, 6: 610. Available at: https://doi.org/10.3389/fpsyg.2015.00610

Walker, L. (2016) A few things moral exemplars have shown me about character, in *Cultivating Virtues: Interdisciplinary Approaches*, Oriel College, Oxford, 7–9 January. Available at: https://www.jubileecentre.ac.uk/userfiles/jubileecentre/pdf/conference-papers/Cultivating_Virtues/Walker%2C%20Lawrence.pdf

Warneken, F. and Tomasello, M. (2008) Extrinsic rewards undermine altruistic tendencies in 20-month-olds, *Developmental Psychology*, 44 (6): 1785–1788.

Weber, M. and Ruch, W. (2012) The role of a good character in 12-year-old school children: Do character strengths matter in the classroom?, *Child Indicators Research*, 5 (2): 317–334.

Weissberg, R.P. and O'Brien, M.U. (2004) What works in school-based social and emotional learning programs for positive youth development, *Annals of the American Academy of Political and Social Science*, 591 (1): 86–97.

Whitney, M.P., Vozzola, E.C. and Hofmann, J. (2005) Children's moral reading of Harry Potter: Are children and adults reading the same books?, *Journal of Research in Character Education*, 3 (1): 1–24.

Wildemeersch, D. (2009) Social learning revisited: Lessons learned from North and South, in A. Wals (ed.) *Social Learning: Towards a Sustainable World*. Wageningen: Wageningen Academic Publishers.

Willemse, M., Lunenberg, M. and Korthagen, F. (2008) The moral aspects of teacher educators' practices, *Journal of Moral Education*, 37 (4): 445–466.

Wimborne, O. (2020) Extending high quality social action into primary schools, *Impact: Journal of the Chartered College of Teaching*. [Online.] Available at: https://impact.chartered.college/article/extending-high-quality-social-action-primary-schools/ (accessed 3 February 2021).

Wright, D., Morris, I. and Bawden, M. (2014) *Character Education: A Taught Course for 11 to 16 Year Olds*. Birmingham: University of Birmingham, Jubilee Centre for Character and Virtues. [Online.] Available at: www.jubileecentre.ac.uk/secondaryprogramme

Wright, J., Warren, M. and Snow, N. (2021) *Understanding Virtue: Theory and Measurement*. Oxford: Oxford University Press.

YouGov (2018) *What Students Want from Their Teachers – YouGov Internal Survey Results Back to School*. Available at: https://yougov.co.uk/topics/education/articles-reports/2018/09/04/what-pupils-want-their-teachers (accessed 3 February 2021).

Index